DENVILLE

········· *in* ·········

WORLD WAR II

PETER ZABLOCKI

for the Denville Historical Society and Museum

THE
History
PRESS

Published by The History Press
Charleston, SC
www.historypress.com

Front cover, top left: courtesy of Mr. Walter Mutz; *top right*: Denville Historical Society; *bottom left*: courtesy of Hank Patterson; *bottom right*: Denville Historical Society.
Back cover: Denville Historical Society; *inset*: Denville Herald.

First published 2021

Manufactured in the United States

ISBN 9781467148955

Library of Congress Control Number: 2020948634

Notice: The information in this book is true and complete to the best of our knowledge. It is offered without guarantee on the part of the author or The History Press. The author and The History Press disclaim all liability in connection with the use of this book.

To Deidra, Lucas and Landon…my world.
—P.Z.

CONTENTS

ACKNOWLEDGEMENTS

Researching World War II began with a conversation with the late president of the Denville Historical Society, Judy McBride, who told me to get myself moving if I wanted to make it to interviewing any surviving members of the Greatest Generation in Denville—and for those who knew Judy, it was not exactly in those words. The first of the many people I interviewed, Mr. Henry Patterson, really awoke in me the desire to tell the story of men and women of Denville who sacrificed so much; and I thank him not only for his service but also for being gracious enough to take the time to speak to me on a few occasions. Similarly, I would like to especially thank the following people who donated their time and energy to share their stories: Russ Darpa, Al Sipple, James Viliard, Walter Mutz, Athena Leonard, Harold Buchanan, Elizabeth Hardy, Winn Hill, Carolyn Chermak, Marion Lester, Joan Knapp, Joan Berg, Fran Lodry, Alvina Baggot, Dolores McDonald and Georgia Cougle.

I would also like to thank Ruth Gimbel for putting me in touch with various veterans and for providing me with her Denville TV files and recorded interviews of other veterans from over the years; she was invaluable to this research. Also, a sincere thank-you to Siobhan Koch for granting me access to the PDF files of the *Denville Herald* and the *Citizen*, which became the basis for this work. Thank you to Roseanne Jones and Geraldine Taormina from the Denville Senior Citizen Center for all their help in getting me in touch with amazing longtime citizens of Denville, who themselves need to be thanked for sharing their stories. Thank you to Megan Roche for granting me the opportunity to create a monthly column in the *Denville Life* about our town's past, which prepared me for this research. And thank you to my editor at The History Press, J. Banks Smither, for his guidance and support through this process.

Last, but certainly not least, thank you to all the men and women who fought in the Second World War. Their sacrifice has not been lost to posterity.

INTRODUCTION

I walked into the Oaks Senior Living Community in Denville, New Jersey, on January 28, 2020, a little apprehensive. I have met and spoken to quite a few World War II veterans in my life as an educator. Yet, here I was, shaking hands with one of the last four surviving D-Day veterans from my hometown of Denville. I was in awe. At the time, I had just concluded writing my book on Denville in World War I. I decided not to waste time and started to actively seek out any remaining World War II veterans from the small Morris County town for my research into perhaps the greatest sequel the world had ever seen. In the end, I managed to interview not only veterans of the great conflict but also numerous citizens of Denville who lived in the town at that time. Together with a plethora of other sources, the invaluable information gained through these interviews allowed me to reconstruct what life in the small town was like between 1941 and 1945. Subsequently, I was able to gather many stories of the town's World War II veterans from both the Pacific and European theaters of the war, many having been published in past editions of the now-defunct *Denville Herald*. There were a few who chose not to relive those times and declined the interview; I respect their decision.

Henry Patterson was still a commanding presence at the age of ninety-six. He shook my hand firmly, introduced himself as Hank and invited me for coffee in the cafeteria. It did not take long after we sat down for Hank to ask me, "So, you want to know a little about my service?" At the time, I did not really know what I was looking for in regards to my research. I started with questions that I had written prior to our meeting. I was more like a sponge wanting to simply absorb as much information as possible. I still have no recollection of when I stopped writing and put my pen down, but I do know that it was not long into the conversation. After getting an "OK" to record the conversation, I sat there in admiration, listening to a humble hero tell his story. I had only written five lines. I know, because I still have my notepad from that day. Meanwhile, I also have nearly three hours of interview recordings with Hank from the two meetings we had in which I simply sat and listened. You will read about his story in the latter section of this book. I was amazed with the sincerity and modesty of this man who was awarded the Legion of Honour, Chevalier, the highest honor awarded by the French government to a non-French citizen, for his actions in World War II. I was also amazed by the way he made everything seem so effortless. After tales of his participation on D-Day—the greatest invasion of World War II—his role in his ship *Quincy*, transporting President Franklin Delano Roosevelt to the Yalta Conference and meeting General Dwight Eisenhower, what really touched me was his story of the one thing that got him through the war: the love for his future wife, Claire. He proudly pointed out that she wrote him a letter for nearly each day he was at sea with the U.S. Navy. "Oh, the letters, when they would come, they would be in a stack this thick [pointing out the numerous-inch thickness with his fingers]….I always knew what was happening back home, and I so badly wanted to be back there with her."

Hank's wife, Claire (Ziegera) Patterson, lived through the war here on the homefront, in the Cedar Lake community of Denville. And while I was not able to meet Claire—she passed away a few months before I met Mr. Patterson—I was able to read her memoirs and see her letters from the time of the war and after. I wish I had gotten to know her, as well. The loving couple and their war story made me completely alter my approach to the research at hand. Their love carried those two through the conflict, one fighting the war in Europe, and the other at home in a small New Jersey town waiting for any news from the front. This made me realize that the tale of Denville and its people in World War II could not be told from the strictly academic perspective of books and past studies. It needed to be told through the eyes of those who lived it. History, and in this case war, is lived just like one's life: one person at a time. Therefore, Denville's story could not simply be another narrative of events; it needed to be a story of its people.

Patterson's account seemed to be in line with what I was finding as I continued meeting people in town who were well into their late eighties and nineties. After interviewing ninety-eight-year-old Walter Metz, a U.S.

Marine who had fought on Okinawa in the Pacific theater, I came to find out that his wife of many years, and another Denville resident, was also a World War II veteran. She unfortunately died as recently as two months prior to our meeting. Her story, learned secondhand from Mr. Metz as well as his daughter, provided yet another layer to the role of the town's citizens in this great conflict. Although she moved to Denville shortly after the war, Helen C. Mutz was a veteran of the war like her husband, having served in the WAC (Women's Army Corps)—just as I came to find out some women of the town had during the war. By the time I sat down with the numerous ladies at the Denville Senior Citizen Center whose husbands had long passed, I came to see Denville's story of what transpired here during the great conflict as one of hope and sacrifice. "We did what we had to do," said Athena Leonard, who was a mere child living in Indian Lake in Denville during the conflict. It did not matter if you were seven or seventy, a man or a woman, a Republican or a Democrat. The war in Denville, as it had across the nation, united people like nothing before it. As the news of my research started to get out in town, I was contacted by numerous people well into their nineties who informed me that it was time for them to share their stories. I spent months conducting interviews, some in person, others over the phone, which gave me the pleasure of getting to know amazing people with amazing stories to tell. I spoke to veterans, war-industry workers and even a British war bride. They all had one thing in common: their hometown (sometimes adopted) of Denville, New Jersey.

I noticed a pattern, a feeling of humble, untouted sacrifice. Yet it was not just that sacrifice. It was more of an "all-in attitude," an almost musketeer-like, "All for one, and one for all." And it was in the same token, business as usual. One did what they knew to be necessary, without having to be prompted. War and the sacrifices that came with it were infused into everyday life. Harold Buchanan recalled to me that as a teen during the war he would go to school at the Denville Main Street School, spend all afternoon collecting for scrap drives with his friends and still make it home to listen to his favorite radio show, *The Lone Ranger*. No one complained, they all did their part, no matter how big or how small. Athena Leonard remembered her father, Robert Matthews, being inducted as a volunteer police officer to the Denville Police Reserves to beef up the force and the town's home defense measures. Like Matthews, people who stayed behind held numerous jobs in the community. Many had more than one—their real job and the various posts they volunteered for, including as air raid wardens, Denville Defense Council members and/or positions on the local draft board. Alvina Baggot and Elizabeth Hardy recalled to me the stamp books, rationing cards and shortages that made everyday life challenging. But Alvina also remembered how none of that detracted from having a great childhood, as her mother always "made do." Of course, "it helped that my mom worked for the Office of Price Administration," she added, chuckling. In fact, women who stayed behind held their households together, often using only the bare necessities. They famously worked in war-related industries, as was the case with Claire Ziegra and Elizabeth Hardy. And yet they still managed to give up the little free time they had left in the day to organize various fundraisers for the Red Cross and/or the Morris County War Chest.

According to the award-winning historian and filmmaker Ken C. Burns, Americans learned how the war was going from three sources; nightly radio reports, local newspapers (there were more than eleven thousand in the country at the time) and the newsreels that preceded movies at local theaters.[1] Lucky for historians today, Denville had its own paper, the *Denville Herald*. Nearly eighty years after, with many people having died, the local newspaper became invaluable to this research and book. Written by those who lived in the community and were passionate about their mission to inform their friends and neighbors, newspaper articles equally highlighted the good and bad sides of humanity during the conflict. The Denville paper did not shy away from any of it, whether it was a baby abandoned in the pew at St. Mary's Church in town around Christmas in 1944 or a car theft in front of Denville's Wayside Inn in May of the same year (the crime was forgiven for the sheer fact that the thief was a man in uniform).

Through the newspapers' classified sections, notes to the editor, mailbag letters and various columns relating to food, rationing, extracurricular activities and men and women in uniform, we get to hear the real-life experiences of individuals who walked the same streets we walk today. Using an analogy of a team of horses working together and accomplishing more than twice as much as any could alone, the *Denville Herald* outlined its mission in the time of war:

> *It's much the same with newspapers and the people of a community. You can have a good community without any newspaper, but you'll have a better community if there is a local newspaper pulling along with the people for their mutual benefit. The will to cooperate, to pull together, must be present on both sides. The people can't force the newspapers to take an aggressive stand in local betterment. The newspaper can't compel the people to take an interest in local affairs. They have to pull together.*[2]

In a similar advertisement, the newspaper proclaimed that everybody's business was their business, an exception to the rule that everybody's business is nobody's business. The editor admitted that he could probably go along quite comfortably and make fewer enemies "by always waiting until at least 51 percent of the public had made up its mind and then following the path of least resistance."[3] But that was not the local paper's job.

Indeed, the *Denville Herald* had a record of being instrumental in reflecting the townspeople's everyday concerns and fostering their much-needed and desired changes. A couple of years prior to the war, the paper publicized the controversial house-numbering initiative in Denville—the town did not have such a system until 1938. Through various mailbag and local editorial pages, the *Herald* made the less enthusiastic citizens see that the rest of the town saw this change as one that was needed for the better good. By wartime, the townspeople appreciated the advantage of an address that could be found without the help of a local guide. Similarly, the paper was instrumental, through its reporting on the numerous automobile accidents in the town's strip of Route 6 (today's Route 46), in getting a white line painted up the center of the road. Without having to push for anything, the newspaper's simple publication of people's concerns and own voices on the problem of the three-lane layout of the highway strip in Denville—by then being referred to as "Death Valley"—impelled the township to make the change. As such, the newspaper's credibility as the voice of the people made it a great source and supplement on which this research relies. Furthermore, local papers such as the *Citizen of Morris County* and the *Morristown Daily Record* have over the years published various articles and interviews with Denville's veterans. These also came in handy when reconstructing their stories for this research.

Similarly, the World War II archive at the Denville Historical Society and Museum contains memoirs, letters and other articles pertaining to the town's history throughout the conflict. Coupled with letters and interviews compiled and conducted by others over the past eighty years, enough light was shed on the topics that still needed to be researched to get a starting point. The last thing that we often take for granted when doing research is the unwritten word—namely, pictures. There are indeed quite a few photos in the collections at the local museum that tell a story of Denville during the war. Many were just waiting to be found in their dusty folders among other pictures of people and their families that have been donated over the years.

As I was leaving Mr. Patterson after our first interview, he stopped me in the door and said that if I remembered anything that he had told me, he wanted me to know just one thing. He proceeded to tell me that when he and his wife had moved to the assisted living community, one of the staff had stopped them in the hallway to tell them how cute it was that they were still holding hands after all those years of marriage. He told her that Claire was his wife, and they have been holding hands through a lot of the good times and all the bad times, for a long time. They were apart throughout the war—so many years ago—and he swore to himself that he would never let her go once he got back. With tears in his eyes he said to me before he closed the door, "She is gone now; so remember son, when you go home, don't take things for granted; hold your wife's hand and never let go; because one day, there will not be a hand to hold, and in life we never know when that will be and whose hand will be left." It really hit me then. After all this man had lived through and done for his nation, it never took away his humility or his love and compassion for others. These heroes were real people. I needed to tell Hank and Claire's stories and others' just like them—the ones who left to fight across the oceans and the ones who stayed back to fight a different kind of war at home.

The following is my research into what has been dubbed by a famous journalist, Tom Brokaw, the "Greatest Generation." It is a story of a town, but perhaps more so of its people. It is a story that transcends a zip code. It is a story of small-town America, where local folks fought the war against the Axis in their own ways. They fought it in their kitchens and gardens, at the gas stations and in the stores, and among friends at work and alone at night in their homes. Apart from the Civil War, the Great Depression, the events of September 11, 2001, and the most recent COVID-19 crisis, World War II is arguably the most traumatic era in our nation's history. This book is about the experiences of those who lived through it. If there ever were any doubts as to how the Greatest Generation earned that title, the stories of men and women that follow can put those to rest. This is Denville's story of World War II, but it could easily be a story of any small town in our great nation.

Part I

OVER HERE

Chapter 1

DENVILLE ON THE EVE OF WAR

ew Jersey was thriving in 1940. The Garden State had found
itself in a favorable economic position in relation to the years of
the Great Depression that closed the previous decade. Although
President Franklin Delano Roosevelt was to say in his speech to Bostonians
on October 30 that "your boys are not going to be sent into any wars,"
that did not mean that the war was not already here in some capacity.[1]
For the Garden State, the war waging since Hitler's forces invaded Poland
in September 1939 had a positive effect. It essentially evaporated any
remnants of the nation's economic depression of the 1930s. War contracts
from England and France were coming in a rate that left the state's factories
fatigued from rushing to keep up with fulfilling the never-ending orders. Yet
the year also saw the first peacetime draft in American history as a measure
of the new national preparedness initiative. As local draft boards began
forming and the inevitable dark cloud of war hung over the nation, the
people of a small New Jersey town in Morris County almost carelessly went
about their business. Denville, a strongly Republican town, as evidenced by
local newspaper editorials and election results from 1940 and 1944, was not
supportive of what it considered FDR's push to bring the nation into the
European conflict. Thus, while the people followed all national and state
regulations and preparedness measures, they did not let the European war
dampen their spirits. It was in essence a calm before a storm, and it was
business as usual. It also placed the small town in line with the rest of the
nation; once the shots were fired, Denville, like the nation as a whole, had to
quickly mobilize and put in a total war effort.

Denville's Imperial Field, where children and adults alike would go to watch local ball games during World War II. Today, it is the site of Morris County Vo-Tech. *Denville Historical Society*.

By January 1940, a total of 433,000 men and women labored in New Jersey's industries, the highest total since World War I.[5] This number only grew as Hitler's forces continued to conquer the European continent and England's military production contracts with the United States grew with its desperate fight for survival. The Garden State's industries provided radios, automobiles, ships, ammunition, uniforms, chemicals, airplane engines, machines, food, gasoline, copper and hundreds of other materials by which war could be conducted.[6] In Paterson, the Curtiss-Wright Corporation built 139,000 aircraft engines, more than any other firm in the county through the duration of the war. The shipbuilders in Camden and Kearny built a quarter of all destroyers delivered to the U.S. Navy.[7] Hoboken's Bethlehem Steel and Todd Shipyards registered nearly 10,000 ships repaired in their shipyards.[8] Not to be outdone, the gasoline makers in Union County, Copper Mines in Middlesex County and iron mines in Passaic and Morris Counties raced to feed the Allied war machine.[9] The *Denville Herald* proudly reported that New Jersey maintained its reputation as the Garden State by leading all other states in the production of many vegetables, fruits and berries for market and canning in 1939.[10] The several New Jersey DuPont powder mills also reopened for operation and explosives makers near Kenvil and Dover added new shifts. While all this industrial growth was relevant to the state, it was the explosives munition plants, due to their proximity, that perhaps most influenced the Denville citizens before the war started.

Many Denville residents alive in the 1940s remember the massive industrial complex of the Hercules Power Plant, located in Kenvil and in Roxbury. It was remembered by residents not just for its sheer size of 1,200 acres and the fact that it employed many locals, but also because of the massive explosion at the plant on September 12, 1940. Condemned as an act of sabotage against the British, the explosion detonated nearly 300,000 pounds of gunpowder and leveled nearly twenty buildings, with shockwaves being recorded as far away as New York City.[11] Fran Lodry, a young girl at the time, remembered her house windows shaking, nearly bursting. Others remember the heavy traffic through the town, as Route 6 running through Denville was the main road between Kenvil and Dover. It was via this route and hence through the center of town that the injured were transferred to the Dover General Hospital.[12] The *Herald* reported that cars of sightseers and relatives of Hercules workers jammed every road for miles around the plant, creating a massive backup as far as Denville. The newspaper also added that every street corner on Route 6 from Kenvil to Dover was packed with people looking west.[13] This level of traffic was not all that unusual, as locals recalled that the highway always jammed on weekends, in turn creating massive traffic in the small town. Denville's Route 6 was one of the only roads heading west out of the state (before the construction of Route 80).[14] It was later reported that fifty-two people had died in the disaster and nearly one hundred were injured. Volunteer police and firemen of Denville were reported to have been among the first responders on the scene, "where many were able to assist in rescuing the dead and wounded from the fire and later explosions."[15] Denville physicians and nurses also gave valuable assistance until the crisis was over.[16]

Howard Dickerson of Denville found himself right in the middle of one of the most infamous events in New Jersey's twentieth-century history. Having worked as a pipefitter at the Kenvil plant, starting three months prior to the explosion, he was lucky to not always be inside the buildings at the plant. As later reported the day of the explosion, he was the only Denville person to be injured, with none being killed. Through his own recollection of events, he was about 350 to 400 feet away from the line where the first blast occurred. He noticed an explosion and fire in the solvent recovery building and turned to run. Several seconds later, the big blast came, and he found himself on the ground. He started to get up and then found that his leg was out of commission. Unable to escape further, and surrounded by a rain of falling debris, he crawled to a pile of lumber, which shielded him a little from the fire. There, he set about making splints for his leg from loose pieces of wood. He was found a few minutes later by plant rescue workers and was taken in an ambulance to Dover General Hospital.[17] As this was one of the first major attacks of sabotage in the state—later proven to have been carried out by a group of German Americans residing in New Jersey's Sussex County on behalf of the Nazi effort against the Allies in Europe—Howard Dickerson was the first Denville casualty of the war. As for Howard's town, the editor of the Denville newspaper used the Hercules explosion to bring attention to another problem specifically plaguing the small Morris County town before the larger issues of war would take its place.

For Denville on the eve of the United States' entrance into World War II, the people had other, more local issues to worry about than what was happening in Europe. "As shocked and grieved as this community is at the terrible price exacted in the Hercules disaster…compare the furor over the loss of fewer than 50 lives as the result of an explosion with our calmness in the face of thousands killed every year on the highways."[18] James Whitton, the editor of the *Herald*, was not wrong in pointing out the eighteen deaths as a result of motor vehicle accidents in Morris County in just that year; and that did not include the countless injuries sustained in other collisions. Denville was at the forefront of this tragedy. Route 6, which cut through the town, witnessed so many accidents that it was dubbed by the locals "Death Valley." The local newspaper really let an image speak louder than words when it plastered a graphic picture of two local youths who had been struck and killed by a motorist on the infamous highway strip on March 21, 1940.[19] The Sunday prior, two young men had been instantly killed and a third miraculously unhurt when the trio walking home along Route 6/Savage Road from the Denville Theatre were struck by an owner of a local business who was arraigned on charges of reckless driving. Just a day after, there was another accident between two cars just a block away from the deadly scene. While no one was mortally wounded, the drivers of both vehicles had to be taken to the local hospital. These events led to a plea from Denville's chief of police: "In the name of the love that all of us bear our little children…[I am] appealing to the parents of Denville to obey…the proper habits of safety on the streets…that we ask the children to follow."[20]

And so, while Denmark and Norway had just fallen to Nazi forces, with France being invaded and the Battle of Britain just a month away, the small town concentrated on typical small-town issues such as traffic accidents and the debates over the need for a house-numbering system. The bickering over the latter, still reported in July of that year, had spanned two years before it was finally settled and agreed on. By 1941, the Works Progress Administration was on its way to cataloging the town's streets and numbering the residents' homes as well as vacant lots. Within months, the people of Denville would have bigger things to worry about.

The conflict now waged nearly all over the world—the Japanese war against neighboring Asian nations, the Germans and Soviets dividing Europe and the Italians attempting to conquer Africa. Yet what was happening "over there" did not deter those bent on committing crimes "over here." There were numerous reports of thefts as well as battery in the months leading up to the U.S. entrance into the war. At one point, one of the more famous taverns in town, located on Route 6, was broken into. Liquor, a cigarette machine and a record player were stolen.[21] Ironically, the tavern's temporary closing was especially rough on local kids. One Denville citizen recalled being brought there with his father to watch baseball games being played on mules on a makeshift field behind the bar.[22] A gas station in Lake Arrowhead was broken into for the third time in a month. Luckily, the owner got smart, taking the money with him each night. The robbers got away with only thirteen cents from the cash register. In perhaps one of the most bizarre thefts of the time, Carl Benner's house was ransacked for the second time in two years, this time the day before Christmas Eve. This would not have been so peculiar had Carl not been the town's Santa Clause and was not acting as such for the Denville Fire Auxiliary's events on both occasions his house was broken into.[23] Ironically, nothing but an electric fridge and unopened Christmas presents were taken. At least the one hundred or so kids who showed up to meet Kris Kringle on Broadway Avenue that night had a good time. Yet, things weren't all bad, all the time. The people of Denville could be proud of many good deeds performed before the sacrifice that was to be asked of them in just a few short months.

Overcome by the sun while looking for berries one Thursday morning, Amelia Hellos found herself spending a day and a night crawling through the brush and swamps off Morris Avenue in Denville in a futile effort to find her way back home.[24] The finding of the nearly seventy-year-old woman was credited to the sixty Denville Boy Scouts who accomplished what the Denville Police and Fire Departments could not, when two boys heard her moaning 1 mile out from her home as they were helping with the search. On another occasion, a missing three-year-old girl from Indian Lake was found just in time by curious folks who saw her admiring movie posters in front of the Denville Theatre on Broadway after she was pronounced missing by her mother that morning. The little girl had apparently walked the 2 miles to the center of town from her house based on her memory of the route she followed with her older brother on their weekly trips to the post office.[25] Another random act of kindness seemed odd even to those living in the 1940s. As a local man helped a couple with some directions when they found themselves on Broadway Avenue. The people of Denville stared in astonishment when they saw a covered wagon drawn by a husky team of oxen trample through the center of town. The *Herald* reported that the historic scene in the modern setting was provided by Mr. and Mrs. Hugh S. Ollson of Warren, Pennsylvania, who were completing the early laps of their 440-mile journey home after a brief sojourn at the World's Fair.[26] It was Mr. Ollson's first trip to New York City on his wagon since 1899. While he thought it was just fine, his wife would have preferred the bus.

Good and bad happenings aside, many residents soon began to see the entrance into the war in terms of "when" instead of "if." To them, the tipping point between the two rested on the results of the 1940 election. War was certainly in the back of the people's minds, even in small towns such as Denville. Following numerous town events for European war relief, including dances and card parties sponsored by the Republican Club at the town's exclusive Wayside Inn, new editorials and mailbag letters began to appear in the local paper about the concepts of war and peace. The conversation about war had most certainly started across the United States. Speaking in front of a packed church, Reverend Wallace G. Sorenson of the Denville Community Church outlined the various fears of the local public and provided the church's stand on the war being waged across the oceans. In his liturgy, he stated that it would be terrible, after having experienced the First World War, for the people of this country to be urging the nation to go into another military hurricane. If not necessarily providing any specific solutions, apart from supporting defense programs and urging everyone to not lose their faith in God, the reverend did hit the nail on the head concerning his constituents' fears and concerns.

> *Fear and hysteria are in the air. The Blitzkrieg across Norway, Denmark, and Low Countries; the conquest of France and the entrance of Italy on the side of Germany, have generated a mounting sense of horror, anger, and dismay in* [our fellow citizens], *Europe is falling to Hitler. Next, he will come over here, is the way many Americans are thinking….We*

must help Britain—we must keep all we have here to defend ourselves—we should send in our entire military and air equipment to the Allies—we should send an expeditionary force to Europe—we should declare war at once—our government is lending aid and comfort to this hysteria in order to keep the nation frightened enough so that new taxes for armaments will not be criticized.

For Denville, a Republican banner was strung over Broadway—the biggest the town had ever seen. The Democratic president, running for an unprecedented third term, would be the decisive factor between peace and democracy, and war.

Months prior to the election, an article in the *Denville Herald* asked the townspeople if they would prefer "ballots now, or bullets later?"[27] The article outlined the issue facing the people in the new election: it was not whether they would elect a man who would not try to be a dictator if he got the chance, but whether they would give him that chance. It was admitted that in his first two terms, FDR had indeed done much that was good; it was also pointed out that his government, with its New Deal and armament measures, was starting to resemble a dictatorship. There was no doubt in the author's mind that reelecting Roosevelt was going to bring the nation to war. Writing months later, the *Denville Herald* editor weighed

Republican banner flying over Broadway during the 1940 election. *Denville Historical Society.*

in on the controversy, publishing a piece outlining how the president was bringing the nation to dictatorship. Comparing the United States to France, Germany, Italy and Mexico, the editorial outlined extravagant public works that concentrated power in the executive, the undermining of an independent judiciary and excessive national debt and conscription—all signs indicating that the nation was going in the wrong direction.[28] Ironically, Whitton also added that the final completion of this dark turn would be realized with nationalizing of industry, regimenting farms and regimenting labor. And although these things were indeed happening, or would happen once the nation entered the war, the United States thankfully did not become anything like some of the nations the editor compared it to. At least to most of the population, that is what it seemed. The national election went to Roosevelt, but all Denville Republicans kept their seats in local government. FDR or not, the war was coming.

Under the direction of New Jersey governor A. Harry Moore, the state's National Guard left for training camps in the summer of 1940 in what was deemed at the time as a preparedness measure. This was followed just a couple of months later, in October of that year, by the first U.S. national peacetime draft. Draftees began leaving before Christmas. Yet, it was all still viewed and treated as a joke instead of grim reality. A New Jersey historian, John T. Cunningham, wrote that the citizen soldiers used broomsticks for guns and cars for tanks, with the rest of the trainings just as unreal. Mockingly, he asked if rookies peeling potatoes at Fort Dix or getting blistered feet in a Texas camp could have any relationship with Europe's war.[29] Denville found itself being swept away with the new wave of national and state preparedness measures. Before conscription, local citizens were urged by various articles outlining the need for young men to join the National Guard. It was viewed and "supported by Governor Moore, State Military Officials, the New Jersey Defense Council, veteran and civic organizations and other agencies as a great patriotic move."[30] The aim was to secure three thousand enlistments in the New Jersey unit. "Our defense requires sacrifice by every one of us which means enlistment of our sons and other male relatives, over the age of 18 years of age, healthy and without dependents," proclaimed the state commander of the American Legion, John A. Whamsley.[31] As editorials point to Denville men not being convinced, it does seem that the conversation about joining the National Guard centered more on the economic perks that would come from doing so. Not forgetting that the United States was still in the long process of getting out of the Great Depression, many small-town Americans were still cautious about their employment status. An enticement that was widely discussed in town was the training certificate one would receive following the one-year mandatory training. To many, this was valuable in securing employment. Anticipating the inevitability of a peacetime draft, A.H.F. Stephan, chairman of the New Jersey Defense Council, said, "Employees will be more interested in hiring men who have had a year's training, rather than those whom might be taken from their employment during the year."[32] Within just a few weeks, the conversation would be null. On September 16, 1940, President Roosevelt signed into law the Selective Training and Service Act of 19 0, enacting the first peacetime draft in the nation's history.

According to the new preparedness measure, all men between the ages of twenty-one and forty-five were required to register with local draft boards; by the time the United States entered the war barely a year later, all men ages eighteen to forty-five were subject to military service, and all men from eighteen to sixty-five were required to register.[33] In a letter to an editor, a Denville citizen acknowledged that conscription was "probably a good thing," albeit a "necessary evil kind of move towards self-defense."[34] He added that "like most everybody in this country," the people of Denville shared his views. Yet at least one other townsman did not share in the fervor, as he questioned the nation's motives in strengthening the national defense through drafting men into military service by the hundreds of thousands and at the same time allowing labor racketeers to disrupt the normal movement of goods through various strikes in the metropolitan area.[35] At the end of the day, it did not really matter how people felt—conscription was a reality. In Denville, Selective Service draft boards were established in the Denville Main Street School, the local library and the firehouse.[36] At each location, the men were greeted by a member of the election board and three local teachers. Teachers not serving on the boards were required to go to school and spend the day there in case they were needed, although school was not in session. Once there, registrants filled out cards with their names, addresses, relatives, employer and place of employment and were classified as to their physical characteristics. Once this was complete, the registrant would be given a questionnaire that asked detailed questions—over thirty on dependents alone—related to supporting claims made for exemption or deferred classification. This of course required legal paperwork in support.[37] These questionnaires were very extensive and overbearing.

In Denville, a separate Draft Advisory Board had to be organized to assist in questionnaire answers for those looking for deferment. A Union Hill resident of Denville supplied the first case for the local board, which met in the town's firehouse on Main Street, when he asked for help with filling out his answers. Priding itself for employing personnel that "represented the whole neighborhood," the board was open for questions and to assist those who needed help from 7:30 p.m. to 9:30 p.m., Monday through Friday.[38] But it was made clear that they were there to assist only. Those who showed up with blank questionnaires were turned away and asked to come back with as much of the document completed as possible. The first Morris County draft quota to be requested by the State Draft Board was easily furnished in late November 1940 and without a single Denville resident. In fact, it took a few months before any Denville boys were called in. Partially responsible for the low numbers of Denville men being drafted before the war was a high number of volunteers form the surrounding towns in the county. This time, it was early volunteers from Dover and Parsippany-Troy-Hills who filled the requested number of twenty-nine men from Denville's district before the U.S. entrance into the conflict.[39] And so, with local draft boards set up and all men registered, life in Denville went back to the new normal.

The first week of December 1941 was not much different from past holiday seasons in downtown Denville, as Christmas shoppers flocked to its numerous boutique-type stores. An ad sponsored by the Denville Chamber of Commerce invited guests to the town's business district with "progressive and attractive" shops. The district, a triangular block arrangement with wide streets and plenty of parking, was advertised as carrying a large variety of merchandise with a wide range of both style and quality.[40] The Fads and Fashions store, proclaimed the "Woman's Shop of Denville," was buzzing with men buying last-minute gifts for their wives. The Denville Camera Shop was equally busy, as everyone picked up film for their cameras to capture their holiday memories. Gardner's Gift Shoppe, a favorite of local children for small gifts and toys, was full of youngsters buying presents for their parents. You couldn't see an empty seat in Anna's Hairdressing's waiting room nor past the long line at E.E. Lysaght's Prime Meats and Poultry Store. Even the usually very busy United Cigar Store seemed busier, as people piled in to pick up candy, gifts and stationery. The annual Christmas party sponsored by the Ladies' Auxiliary of the Undenominational Church in the Patriotic Order Sons of America Hall was once again well attended.[41] Following an hour of games, refreshments were served, with each attendee receiving a gift before they departed. The Dickerson's General Store on Route 53 once again won the best holiday window display, for the third year in a row.[42] The holidays were indeed in full swing.

As Denville citizens went to sleep on Saturday night, December 6, 1941, a large American flag flew high above the Main Street's firehouse. Jim Lash, a local landowner and businessman, had donated money for what was called a "mammoth American flag all in lights," to be flown and lit up each year for all in town to see.[43] By the evening of the next day, the flag would be at half-mast. This was to be the happiest holiday since the beginning of the Great Depression a decade earlier. Between the summers of 1940 and 1941, New Jersey received nearly 10 percent of all prime Allied contracts, topped only by California and New York. As the first snow fell on the state in early December, the mood was bright and light. People were at work, and wages were high.[44] As Denville men and women were finishing their Sunday services at one of the few churches in town on December 7, far to the west in Hawaii, a Denville native, Edward J. Stafford, woke up to loud explosions all around him and alarm sirens screaming throughout his ship, USS *Pyro*. He had been stationed at Pearl Harbor for two months. His mundane job on the ammunitions ship had suddenly become too much for even him to handle, but handle it he did. By the end of the day, the young man had become part of a crew that was credited for shooting down a Japanese plane, earning them one Battle Star. Stafford never spoke about that day nor about the following years serving on a hospital ship, USS *Samaritan*, where he witnessed the real carnage of war. It was not until nearly a decade after his death in 1983 that the Denville VFW learned of his involvement at Pearl Harbor and held posthumous special services for him at the Denville cemetery where he is buried.[45]

The Japanese fighter planes departing Pearl Harbor after having dropped their payloads on the unsuspecting U.S. Naval forces had ushered in a new era in American history. "I was riding my bike in Indian Lake [Denville] when I heard someone walking out of their home and yelling that the United States was just attacked and we were going to war. I rushed home as quickly as I could," recalled Harold Buchanan, who would turn nine years old the next day.[46] It would be a birthday he would never forget. People returned home from church and turned on their radios, hearing announcers screaming puzzling names of faraway places most Americans had never heard of. They did manage to catch "Japan" and "sneak attack." The mood in town turned into a combination of fear, confusion and, oddly, eagerness and excitement. Kids ran around outside talking about how the United States was going to get back at the Japs and kill Hitler as young men throughout the town were

Inside the St. Francis Chapel in Denville, where Alvina Baggot heard German Nuns sing on the night of December 7, 1941. *Denville Historical Society.*

making up their minds to join the military instead of waiting to be inevitably called up by their local draft boards. That night, a young Alvina Baggot went to church with her mother and father at St. Francis Chapel in Denville. As the world awaited President Roosevelt's declaration of war the next day, the fifteen-year-old Alvina stood in a pew surrounded by numbers of others listening to the German Catholic nuns' rendition of "Silent Night," sung in German. As she was losing herself in the beautiful performance of the song, she could not help noticing the irony. The next day, the United States was at war with Japan, followed by a declaration of war with Germany three days later. Like so many others in that chapel, the young girl wondered if she would ever hear the nuns sing their German songs again.

Chapter 2

DEFENDING OUR HOMES

People of all ages living in the United States on Sunday, December 7, 1941, knew they had just witnessed a turning point in their nation's history. No matter the age of the person, the moment was not lost on them. The attack would be used as a constant reminder of the sacrifices they would be asked to endure. For Anna Armbruster, Pearl Harbor was all the more significant, as the attack took place on her seventy-seventh birthday. The Denville resident had only two years to live when she penned the following poem a few weeks after the ghostly attack.

And can we forget that night
Where from the star strewn heavens
Foul treachery cast its blows
And struck with all its hideous force
On sleeping families?
And while the envoys so blindly dealt
With lies on their lips
And hypocrisy in their hearts
Their armament on land and sea
Was on its way of destruction.
Never was our eagle so enraged
When looking down from his lone watch
He saw the blasting death
That felled our soldiers stealthily
And then scrammed away, victorious.

For so they think, never can victory come
From such base methods
For when we strike, as stealthy as they
We only pay them back in their own coin
'Tis then they will remember Pearl Harbor
To their undoing.[47]

A short film of the bombing of Pearl Harbor was projected for those interested at the Denville Community Methodist Church.[48] The single showing had to be extended for a week because of the demand. Like Mrs. Armbruster, to whom this was déjà vu (she had lived in the town during World War I), the citizens of Denville would not shy away from the momentous events before them. Concurrent with the draft boards, volunteer enlistments and going-away parties for servicemen being planned by various town organizations, the overall attitude of the townspeople had shifted. Specifically, for a noncombatant American, the Japanese attack had destroyed the long-standing belief in the impregnability of the nation's borders and shores.

The December attack really drove home the new reality that airplanes launched from aircraft carriers could strike the American heartland. German submarines lurking off the East Coast could not only sink U.S. transport ships but also attack major American ports. *LIFE* magazine of March 2, 1942, published a piece detailing President Roosevelt's actions within the first months of the (now American) war. What was striking to those at the time was FDR's proclamation that "the enemy ships could shell New York City tomorrow night as enemy bombers might bomb Detroit." Pressed by a reporter if the U.S. Army and Navy were prepared to deal with any attack, he could not give any guarantees.[49] Americans were now in the fight for their lives, the president stated. The magazine published another article in which it outlined with detailed maps the "Six Ways to Invade U.S." It was stated that "Axis Powers [could] try it if they combined fleets, to win sea superiority."[50] There was no denying the fact, perhaps more so within the first year of the war than in the later years, that fear of an enemy attack on the U.S. mainland really affected people living in the coastal states. In Denville, as in other locations across New Jersey and the nation, this fear prompted citizens to volunteer their assistance in creating and then leading civil-defense efforts. By serving as air wardens, firefighters, plane spotters, security guards and myriad other positions, those left behind on the home front were also able to attain a sense of participation in the war.[51]

Within weeks of the U.S entrance into World War II, Denville organized the Denville Local Defense Council, which was to serve the area for the duration of the war. "Every civilian is a member of the unorganized militia for the common defense," said Colonel William McKinely of Jersey City, principal speaker at the civil-defense rally sponsored by the Denville Local Defense Council at the Denville School on Main Street.[52] One of many such rallies in town sponsored by the organization, this one perhaps best summarized the importance of civil defense, even in a small town. And for any doubters in the crowd, the speaker added, "Modern war involves civilian areas, once considered non-combatant, and requires civilians to know how to take care of themselves through passive defense." Colonel McKinely went on to explain "that while Denville is of no military importance in itself, it is important as a section of the Port of New York defense area."[53] He then went on to point out that the Garden State was a byway of military defense for the northeastern United States and that "all European General Staff plans for the invasion of the U.S. have been based upon penetration of the St. Lawrence and Hudson River valleys, with landing on the Jersey coast as a prelude to the Southern attack."[54] The program of civilian defense was necessary to ensure, at the least, complete calm and self-control on the part of the townsfolk when and if a bombing or invasion test should come—or the dreaded real thing.

People were encouraged to look out for any suspicious activity that might be part of any saboteur initiatives. In Denville, all aliens—that is, persons of German, Italian or Japanese heritage—had been notified by Police Chief Harry B. Jenkins to turn in any cameras, radio transmitting sets or short-wave radio receiving sets in their possession. This order was in accordance with FDR's Executive Order of December 8, 1941, and was being put into effect by local police departments throughout the nation.[55] The property being collected was not to be confiscated, but was simply being held until it could be returned to the original owners. It was later reported by Chief Jenkins that many of the Denville citizens of the singled-out nationalities chose to dispose of their contraband in other ways rather than show up at the town's collection center on the specific date and face the judgment of those waiting to see them. In fact, the town's police headquarters at the firehouse on Main Street was very quiet on the evening of January 12, 1941, when the collection was to take place. Chief Jenkins later admitted that many people had contacted him earlier about disposal methods. "At any rate, it is not our responsibility now. It is up to them if they get caught from now on with anything in their possession that

Downtown Denville during World War II. *Denville Historical Society.*

has been prohibited," he said.[56] For many, the fix was as simple as having their radios converted so they could not receive short-wave messages. On being shown the proper receipt, the Denville Defense Council would grant a permit for usage of the said alien.

When a mass flight of about fifty four-motored American planes flew over the Denville Center after the nation was firmly involved in the world conflict, the *Herald* was quick to point out how "everybody…[now had] a slightly better idea of what the people of Europe have had to endure."[57] Yet it was quickly acknowledged that this was but a "painless" sample. James Whitton, the editor of the paper, best summarized the sentiment. "But the sensations of wonder, awe, and half fear that they inspired, with the roar of their engines and the sight of so many enormous machines overhead, make it a little easier for us in Denville to imagine what it must be like to have, not half a hundred of our own planes humming peacefully past us, but more than 1,000 enemy planes, showering sudden death and worse, droning over us as the target."[58] There was no need to further spur the citizens into defensive measures; they got the point.

The newly established Denville Defense Council had many responsibilities—not just for Denville, but also for Rockaway Borough and Rockaway Township, to which they were designated by the State of New Jersey to relay warnings to. The first step was securing a dedicated twenty-four-hour telephone line, as all emergency calls in town up to that point had been relayed to Chief Jenkins's home/police line. He could not be there answering calls in all hours of the day, as he was out and about the town. This made a call center a necessity. In case of emergency, three casualty stations were established and equipped, at the Denville School, the Community Church and the Union Hill Chapel. Each location had station wagons and light trucks assigned to them to serve as emergency ambulances in case of bombings or attacks. Dr. E.J. Evans, a public health and sanitation chairman, reported that 150 Denville citizens had taken the standard first-aid course, with squads having been selected to man the stations as well as rooms in private homes that had been graciously made available by the townsfolk.[59] By the time of the second ever public meeting in Denville, over 200 people turned out at the Denville School to hear about the council's actions. Many in the crowd wore the armbands of auxiliary forces. About 170 air wardens were put in place across the ten zones the township had been divided into. An additional 40 men joined the police reserves and had taken the prescribed training course.[60] This was certainly beginning to look like a homefront, and the town's citizens began to resemble home soldiers.

It was through the Defense Council's control center, occupying a space above the Lysaght's food store on Main Street, that the people were told how to prepare for the presumed attacks. It was also through the council that they were given the means to do so. The space in the center of town was manned by someone twenty-four hours a day, seven days a week. It contained five separate telephone lines and a system of switches governing sirens throughout the town. It was also the main meeting place for its board, where it would come up with plans for protecting the public. In the two schools in town—with the Denville (Main Street) School boasting having more persons under one roof for longer than any other building in town—plans were put into place and drills implemented to prepare for an attack. At the Main Street School, students would gather in the hallways, which were protected from the outside by two masonry walls. At the Union School, students practiced a complete evacuation, as there was no place safe from glass.[61] The drill saw the students go into the Union Hill Chapel's basement, directly across the street. Luckily, all three of the buildings mentioned— as was the case with the whole town and most of the nation—were never

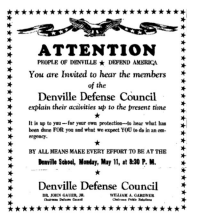

****

ATTENTION

PEOPLE OF DENVILLE ★ DEFEND AMERICA

You are Invited to hear the members
of the

Denville Defense Council

explain their activities up to the present time

★

It is up to you — for your own protection---to hear what has been done FOR you and what we expect YOU to do in an emergency.

★

BY ALL MEANS MAKE EVERY EFFORT TO BE AT THE

Denville School, Monday, May 11, at 8:30 P. M.

★

Denville Defense Council

DR. JOHN GAUER, JR.   WILLIAM A. GARDNER
Chairman Defense Council   Chairman Public Relations

****

Ad for the Denville Defense Council demonstration. *From the* Denville Herald, *May 7, 1942.*

attacked and never had to implement the plans in an actual situation. They still stand in town to this day.

The people were also urged to check their flashlights on a regular basis to ensure their operation when needed in case of an attack. Speaking of attacks, the Denville Defense Council, working with the Denville Road Department, distributed "sand throughout the township…so every home [could] be supplied with material for fighting incendiary bombs," announced the local paper.[62] People were urged to leave pails in front of their homes; trucks covered every street and road and filled every pail or box placed on the curb. As an incentive to cooperate, air wardens conducted random check-ins to make sure that each house was supplied; those found to be negligent would be issued a warning. Of course, not everyone was happy about the militarized state of affairs. Numerous letters to the editor of the *Herald* aired displeasure with the council's methods. On one occasion, the matter was addressed by one of the town's chairmen: "The wardens are not trying to [force you into anything] nor to pry into personal affairs when they ask for information about houses and the inhabitants [and their actions], but are trying only to get the facts which may be needed in case of bombing or other disaster."[63] Although not everyone liked it, the people of Denville did follow and support their Defense Council throughout the war.

The main concern to be addressed by local Defense Councils was the constant threat of a potential attack from the air, at least in the first year of the war. To combat this, each town, Denville included, assigned and trained special air wardens, whose job was to coordinate events on the ground in case of an attack and, more importantly, be the spotters of any incoming attacks that might occur. The impetus was to urge people to act before the bombs started falling and thus minimize the damage that might incur from them. While the *Denville Herald* ran a picture editorial outlining how to distinguish the nationality of aircraft, with hints of what to look for, it was up to the designated air raid spotters to distinguish Axis planes from those of the Allied nations. Those civilians who volunteered for the service were shown films on spotting aircraft, with the Denville Theatre lending its screen for such purposes throughout the war. To raise funds for air raid spotters, the wardens did not rely on the local council's budget as did their bigger brother, the Denville Defense Council. Most of the supplies needed were donated and/or bought with money raised through fundraisers. The Rock Ridge air raid wardens held successful square dances at the popular Fireside Restaurant in town; all profits would be used to buy equipment.[64]

Actively seeking funds for Denville's air raid volunteers was the deputy warden for the town, S.R. Sofield, a World War I veteran and Purple Heart recipient. He witnessed the carnage of war during his time in France and knew what was at stake. What he needed was the backing of his fellow townsfolk to help him protect them. Using the advertising pull of the Defense Council, the Denville air raid wardens were able to procure from the citizens of the town the needed items entirely from donations. These included "heavy raincoats, 2,200 feet of half inch rope and stands to hold it up, warning flags and material for them, steel helmets, heavy gloves, stirrup pumps, axes, smoked glasses." This was supplemented by the council adding "33 zone warden signs, warden's report forms, gas masks, and gas protective suits, flashlights and batteries, first aid kits, gas alarm devices, and logbooks."[65] Once again, the people of Denville came through. Between sending their loved ones overseas to fight, rationing and buying war bonds, the people of the small town still managed to give what they could in order to keep themselves and their neighbors safe. "Help Your Warden," proclaimed headlines in the local paper. "Work with your Air Warden, not against him…; he is not running around because he likes it, but because it's his part in the job that we should all help into the best of our ability." The nearly two hundred official air observers in town worked through the day and night in what the U.S. Army called a national civilian effort "that would otherwise occupy about 100,000 soldiers, and that one airplane with the help of information contributed by the observers is the defense equivalent of 10 planes dependent upon what the pilots can ace for themselves."[66] In order to avoid unnecessary calling in of trainers and transports above them, Sofield used the army-prescribed "WEFT" system of identification in his lectures and certification programs, which he held at Rockaway High School for those interested in joining. Namely, the principal characteristics and features of wings, engine(s), fuselage and tail were noted in logbooks, which then determined if an alarm should be called.

As for all New Jersians, air raids and blackouts became a reality for Denville citizens within a few weeks of the attack on Pearl Harbor in December 1941. On February 1, 1942, at precisely 12:00 p.m., the people of the small town

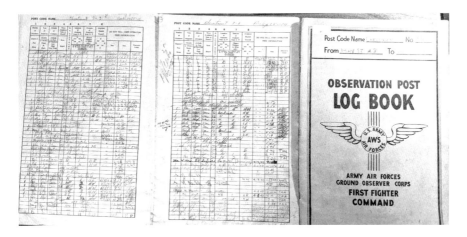

Observation Post Logbook from the Denville Post named "Chestnut," now displayed at the Denville Museum. *Denville Historical Society.*

could not escape the maiden effort of their town's air raid warning signal. The siren, which was purposely scheduled for Saturday so as not to disturb the workweek, went off at peak volume for two minutes, cut off for five seconds and then ran up to the peak for one or two more minute-long blasts; after a pause, there was a single two-minute blast that indicated all clear.[67] A new reality came in loud and clear for all of Denville's townsfolk; they were at war and needed to prepare for the "what if?" Posters appeared around town describing what to do in case an air raid went off. People at home were told to shelter in place and turn off all stove burners; those in a car were to park it and enter the nearest building. If bombs began dropping and the person was unable to reach a building, they were to lie down and protect the back of their head.[68] People were reminded to never shout, scream or run, even if others around them were doing so. The point stressed by the wardens was to avoid a panic that was as dangerous as the bombs themselves. And, above all, when hearing an air raid warning, one was, under no circumstance, to use the telephone. The lines were connected to the system set up to spread warnings and get reports back to defense centers. They could not be taxed by civilian calls that might back up operators and switchboards.[69]

During the first two years of the war, Denville and its people had to get used to numerous air raids, most of them unannounced. As per a poster that hung at the Denville Post Office at the time and is currently on display at the Denville Historical Society's museum, we learn that there were two air raid signals people had to remember. Red signal, meaning "danger immediate," was a fluctuating note of siren or short blasts of factory whistles for three minutes. The white signal, meaning "all clear," was three steady one-minute blasts interspersed by two minutes of silence.[70] On the evening of September 22, 1942, Denville citizens had quite a scare when the air raid system malfunctioned and sent a red signal blasting through the town, shut off eastern radio stations and sent civilian defense staff running to their posts.[71] "Did it give you a little shivery feeling and the thought 'Maybe this is it?'…Did the idea of bombs landing in your block, maybe on your house, seem suddenly more real than when we were simply practicing?" asked the *Herald's* editor. Thankfully, the all-clear signal came through directly after the danger-immediate one, so people did not really have that much time to panic. It was reported that, although brief, the event showed the people's composure and ability to follow directions.

The same could not be said of the October 2 red signal air raid, which, this time, did not turn off immediately. In fact, the all-clear did not come through until 10:37 p.m., after the initial siren went off a little after 8:00 p.m. that evening. Although this time it was an unannounced test, things did not go as smoothly for Denville as one might have hoped. It was reported that in several instances, lights were left on in homes in which no one was around to turn them off. In other homes, where windows were closed and radios were playing, the siren was not heard, and air raid wardens had to scramble to notify the residents to black out.[72] Concurrently, several key members of the local defense organizations could not be located by telephone, and Chief Jenkins was alone in the control center when the red signal came through. Yet not all went wrong that night. Jenkins was able to secure help from the fire reserves meeting in the firehouse basement to black out windows. The first-aid personnel reported to the casualty stations on time—apart from those at the Denville School, who had some delay in getting inside owing to a mix-up about the key.[73] The reason for the late "all clear" was due to the Dover relay officer forgetting to call Denville. Overall, the test went well. By 1943, with the threat of air raids slightly diminishing, the state created a new blue warning signal. The purpose was to permit quicker mobilization of civilian defense personnel and minimize time loss and interference with essential war production and transportation. For the remainder of the war, the blue signal would come on first, before the red, warning of the probability of an enemy air raid and enemy planes appearing to be headed in the town's direction; in other words, get ready.[74] These changes mostly allowed things to go on as normal once the alarm was sounded, instead of residents going into full panic

Air raid poster that once hung at the Denville Post Office. It is now displayed at the Denville Museum. *Denville Historical Society.*

mode or not being prepared for the red, as had happened in Denville during the unannounced drill. Under the blue signal, the civil defense forces mobilized, and home and business lights were blacked out; but pedestrians could proceed, cars could move on with low beam lights and, most importantly, war production could go on. By the second drill, barely a month after the changes went into effect, Denville was commended for its organization and implementation of defense measures during air raid drills by the Denville Civilian Defense Organization and Chief of Police Harry Jenkins.

Apart from air raids, the small town was also subject to blackout restrictions and blackout drills, which came with various degrees of success. The first blackout drill in Denville took place on Tuesday, April 28, 1942, starting at 10:00 p.m. and lasting for fifteen minutes.[75] All air raid wardens, police and fire reserves, emergency medical units, demolition, rescue, and repair squads and all other protective units were ordered to be at their posts half an hour before the blackout began. When the siren sounded, street and highway lights and illuminated traffic signs were turned off and all traffic was stopped, with vehicles ordered to pull off to the side and their lights turned off.[76] Similar regulations were directed to all businesses and homes in Denville, where all gas stations and houses were ordered to turn off their lights. Those caught not following these orders by monitoring air wardens were issued warnings. Dr. John Gauer, chairman of the Denville Local Defense Council, jubilantly reported to the State Defense Council later that night that Denville had come through its first blackout test with a record just under 100 percent perfect.[77] It was noted that with the exception of one house, all homes in the township had been blacked out within a few seconds of the siren's sounding.

There must have been no doubt of the first blackout's success. Mrs. Charles Wertheim, chairman of the Red Cross canteen corps, directed the pre-prepared serving of coffee, cake and donuts to the men as they returned to the firehouse to report.[78] During subsequent blackouts, the worst thing to happen to the township was the numerous car accidents occurring as a result of the drills. The first such accident occurred on the infamous Route 6 strip of Denville, where a car hearing the siren came to a sudden stop, resulting in a three-automobile crash with two cars directly behind it. Although citizens of the state were often warned that a statewide blackout would be held during a given week, they were never told the exact day and time, resulting in many people still finding themselves on the road during the drill. This happened to Mrs. Willie M. Craford, who was visiting a friend in Lake Arrowhead in Denville when she stopped in obedience to the air raid warning on Route 6, only to be struck by a tractor trailer unable to stop in time. While in the end she was reported to be in good condition, her initial injuries resulted in her being taken to Dover General Hospital.[79] One did not need to go outside to get hurt in a blackout; there were plenty of opportunities to do so at home. An investigation by an insurance company at the time uncovered many instances of broken fingers, toes and even noses. It appeared that once all the lights were out, people did not know their way around their houses as well as they thought they did. A new argument even appeared in the *Herald* for having a blackout room in each home, "so one could save their bones from being broken."[80] In the end, the broken toes due to blackouts became just another sacrifice in a long list of efforts asked of the public.

Chapter 3

WASTE NOT, WANT NOT

O nce the war started, the United States found itself having to make up for shortages of critical materials, and it once again turned to its people for help. Although most citizens donated what they could to the war effort, the government asked them for even greater sacrifices. To pay for the enormous cost of the war—nearly $200 billion—the federal government imposed a 5 percent surcharge, or "Victory Tax," on all income taxes.[81] Within a mere month of America's entry into the global conflict, it had also established the Office of Price Administration to ration scarce items and hold inflation at bay by controlling prices. For Denville citizens, as for many across the nation, it was rationing that became probably the peskiest part of the government's civil defense initiatives. Yet all complaining aside, the people of the small Jersey town accepted the system as fair. For the majority, complying with the rationing regulations seemed the least they could do. Reverend Charles Mead, the principal speaker at the dinner in the firehouse given for Denville youths entering service, looked down from the podium at those gathered and proclaimed, "There is no question about the way those in the armed forces contribute…[but] the responsibility of those on the home front to do their share needs to be stressed." As heads in the audience nodded, and families of those sitting in the middle that would soon be off to war murmured whispers of approval, the reverend closed his speech with an audacious, "the home front must perform its part in winning this war!"[82] And perform it, it did.

The government-popularized slogan "Use it up, wear it out, make it do, or do without" became the guiding principle for most citizens.[83] There were many visible changes in Denville due to the shortages brought on by war. Perhaps none was as stressful in the winter months as the quickly depleting coal and furnace fuel oil reserves. Within a few weeks after Pearl Harbor, the town's fire department began offering courses on how to properly use anthracite coal to obtain most heat from the fuel being used. A concerned citizen wrote to the *Denville Herald* that his house's temperature had to be lowered from 68 to 60 degrees and his "family could certainly feel the difference." A town oil supplier and resident, who chose to remain anonymous, called the shortages and government reaction to them "asinine." Namely: "I drive a 12-ton truck all over the town delivering oil in 50 and 100 gallon lots into tanks that could take 500 to 1,500 gallons. I am forced to make four or five trips, burning up rubber, gasoline, and vehicle, where one trip should be enough."[84] The complaints became irrelevant by the second winter, when the issue evolved from not getting enough oil or coal to sometimes not getting any at all.

The Denville School Board decided to close schools from December 23, 1942, to January 25, 1943, as a necessity stemming from not having enough oil to heat the buildings. In lieu of the closing, the students had to make up some of the days by going to school on days that they would normally have off, such as Presidents' Day or Easter break. To make up the lost days that year, school was eventually extended to June 30 from the planned June 15. It became a foregone conclusion when the nationally established Office of Price Administration (OPA)—designed to regulate nearly every aspect of civilian life—put in place a 10,000-gallon annual limit on heating oil. As the Denville schools were using 28,000 gallons, they were forced by the OPA to convert to coal.[85] Faced not only with a lack of fuel oil or the coupons needed to acquire it—and the OPA's order for conversion of non-dwelling oil-burning units—the Denville Fire Department Association was also forced to convert the furnaces at the firehouse into coal-stoker units. Of course, these mandates created their own set of problems. As reported by the *Herald*, the demand for coal outpaced its supply, leading many people in the town to lament the price of fifteen dollars a ton—a 100 percent increase from prewar years. Concurrently, many people who once faced shortages of oil now found themselves lacking the proper amount of coal to heat their homes. In a letter to the editor in late 1943, a Denville citizen called it a "coal famine," adding that the inability to stock up on coal ahead of the winter season was preposterous.[86]

The Denville School on Main Street, circa 1960s. Visible in the front is the Denville Memorial Plaque with the names of those from Denville who had lost their lives in American foreign wars. *Denville Historical Society*.

Through the winter of 1944, children in town would wake up running into their living rooms to turn on the radio station, WOR, to hear their principal, William E. Davenport of the Denville School, make one of his announcements. The administrator would go on the local radio daily to announce if there was enough coal to heat the school and if it would be open for the day.[87] "We missed it by 44 minutes Tuesday [January 18, 1944]…I was ready to announce that noon [for the next day] a shutdown until further notice," recalled the principal.[88] Luckily, in the last hour before the deadline, a supply delivery showed up with part of the five tons of soft coal they were able to procure for the school from another dealer. As the winter went on, the specially formed Denville Emergency Coal Committee was able to secure fifteen additional tons of coal for the township through its visit to the Tamaqua mine in Pennsylvania.[89] In fact, the deal it struck would not only ensure no more disruptions in the delivery of coal for the small town, but within a few months, it also allowed its citizens to once more be able to order their coal supply ahead of the 1945 winter season. The committee explained that the biggest factors for Denville's shortage of coal were the failure of mines to produce enough, railroad companies not always being willing to transport it and the limits placed on dealers by the OPA of the amount of stock they could hold. By going directly to the mines with their pleas and "some political pressure," town officials were able to also "persuade the railroads" and procure the desperately needed coal for their small town.[90] The committee's tenacity also saved the Denville businesses, as they had announced mandatory closings each Wednesday through the winter in order to conserve coal. In the end, no such closings were needed.

As war production increased, there were fewer products available for purchase to the main street consumer. Created by the Roosevelt administration, the Office of Price Administration's purpose was to fight inflation with the freeze of wages, prices and rents. Yet it was the other role of the administration that became controversial. The OPA's rationing program was divided into two categories. First, it limited the purchase of certain commodities that were deemed nonessential. These included tires, cars, metal typewriters, bicycles, stoves and rubber shoes. Second, the quantity of goods allowed to be purchased was limited by quotas. These included butter, coffee, sugar, cooking fat, gasoline and nonrubber shoes (or the type of shoes that citizens could buy).[91] All of the above did not include the other accommodations that the people came to rely on. Much of American factory production had shifted gears toward war, creating shortages in nearly every aspect of desired consumer products. The *Denville Herald* reported on various hacks so that local citizens could make do without. "Do Not Destroy Your Old Mattress!" screamed one headline, "we can show you how to rebuild them equal to new."[92] Others provided advice and patterns for making clothes: "It's Patriotic to Use Up Remnants" and "Patchwork Effects Are Now Popular."[93] In a letter to the editor, one Denville man pointed out how "shortages show inequalities, greed and graft that results in time of great demand and increased purchasing power when a scarce commodity goes unrationed."[94] His peeve: cigarettes. "Some favored few in town, who have an inside track to the supply of the wholesaler or corner drug store, always seem to have plenty of smokes. The rest of us go without because of those who stock up and hoard."

By June 1943, the Newark headquarters of the Office of Price Administration, with the help of thirteen thousand volunteer high school teachers, mailed out fifty-four tons of ration books to all New Jerseyans. Members of the Denville School faculty were deeply indebted to four very patriotic mothers for "attractive and delicious lunches" served to them during their four days of rationing work in March of that year. The specific ladies organized the menus, prepared, delivered and served the food in an effort to make the "trying days as convenient, economical, and pleasant as possible for the teachers."[95] Once the citizens received their coupon books,

National Food Store on Main Street in Denville as it appeared in World War II. *Denville Historical Society*.

they knew their spending habits would change. The OPA rationed twenty essential items, everything from sugar to gasoline. Red point coupons were issued for meat, butter and fats; blue points for canned and processed foods. Gas restrictions were even more elaborate, with drivers assigned a priority distinction between A (General Public) and E (Emergency Vehicle), with gas coupons issued accordingly.[96] The stickers with the assigned letter indication had to be affixed to the car's windshield, determining the driver's gas allowance and freedom to travel at specific times. Taking this a step further, the government also limited the nationwide speed limit to thirty-five miles per hour and prohibited for-pleasure driving as a rubber- and gas-saving measure. It was the latter restriction that sometimes provided humor in the grim times Americans had suddenly found themselves in. Police inspectors in Denville had to listen to the driving public explain why they were out on a pleasure ride on a Sunday afternoon with the wife and the back seat full of kids. Some of the stories they heard were quite imaginative.

A Denville volunteer police inspector tasked with monitoring the Route 6 highway strip running through the small town had many stories to share about people's creativity in trying to get away with driving during rationing. He admitted that of the thirty or so people he stopped in the month of February 1943, "none had the candor to admit that they were just out for a ride." Excuses always ranged from the feebly made up to ingenious, the inspector said in an interview. The beginning of the conversation was always the same: "Let me see your ration book, please," a quick glance and perhaps a request for "Your 'A' book, too, please." It was what came back at him that was often different. A week prior, he had stopped a car with two couples in it. The driver said he was in the moving business and was going to Boonton, where he'd moved a family from Virginia a few days ago. "I damaged his radio and forgot to give him his lawn-mower," the driver said. "So, I am taking a radio repair man," indicating the man beside him, "and the push reel lawn mower," which was indeed squeezed in the back with the handle sticking up between the two smiling women.[97] "Go ahead," was what the police officer had said; it indeed was a creative story. But not all rule breakers fared the same. A "pretentious, young manufacturing executive," riding in a car with his wife, mother and two children, was issued a fine when he argued with the officer that he had the right to "drive to Denville to visit the head of the firm's New York plant," because "there were some things to discuss which couldn't be done over the phone."[98] The same fate met another two young couples who said they were going to inspect their summer cottages in town to shut off the water for winter.

The inspector was kind enough to inform them that winter was over in two weeks and they were a bit late.

Jokes aside, gas-rationing shortages really were a problem for Denville and the nation. Ironically, gas rationing initially had less to do with gas and more to do with tires, as Japan had all but stopped the supply line of rubber to the United States. The Denville tire-rationing board, led once more by Police Chief Jenkins, met with ten tire dealers in the township in January 1942 to outline the seven-classification program for the ability to purchase tires. Unless one could prove that the tires were going on a vehicle operated by a doctor or a nurse, ambulances, fire, police, sanitation or public transportation services, he/she was simply out of luck. Even then, if tires were needed for the approved vehicles, they still had to be inspected by the town tire inspector, in this case Joseph Wolf of the Denville Garage on Main Street. Once all the proper paperwork was completed, Joe would "look at the tires to see whether they deserve recapping or retreading, or whether a complete new tire should be put on."[99] In the latter case, a proper certificate needed to be issued. The whole process could take a couple of months. Of course, every other class vehicle would have to get along with the tires now on the wheels or get retreads or recapped tires. Gas coupons mandated by the OPA were simply a means to discourage driving, not so much to restrict gas usage but to make the tires last for the people and institutions deemed necessary to the war effort.

The tire conundrum had visible effects on the town as well as on the town's businesses, namely the gas stations, service centers and car dealers. It also showcased the typical "buy now, because it may be gone" frenzy we still see to this day when a shortage or a disaster becomes eminent. "Twenty five percent of cars will be off the roads in our town within three months," predicted Joseph Wolf of the Denville Garage within a month after Pearl Harbor.[100] His competitor across the street, Reynolds Dodd of the Texaco station, disagreed. "I expect the situation to ease up a little after the first frenzy is over," he said. "It's the same people creating this [shortage of tires] as who go around buying sugar two pounds here and two pounds there when they've got maybe 50 pounds stored up at home." In the end, they were both right. Those who purchased ahead wound up with a larger supply, but by mid-1942, with stringent OPA restrictions, there was no supply to buy. Similarly, the number of drivers had dropped, perhaps due to the larger number of young men being drafted, who themselves were the principal drivers on the roads. Other businesses, like tire retreading and maintenance services, benefited from rationing. Retreading, which involved using a hot iron spike to cut within and deepen the grooves in tires, nearly doubled in price from thirty cents to fifty cents. Similarly, as new car production had ceased, Wolf admitted that people were a little more careful with their cars, knowing they would have to run them a lot longer. This led to an upswing in car maintenance. Allen's Service Station, another business in town, reported a noticeable increase in the number of motor tune-ups. Charles Spencer of Spencer's Esso Station proclaimed himself lucky with the business of selling recapped (used) tires, which he was able to increase in price from fifty cents each to seventy-five cents and still be the best deal in town.[101] Unfortunately for him, his competition, Kenneth Stevens of the Sinclair station, was right when he said that even the recapped tires would be rationed, with defense workers getting first choice. There was no good way to spin this; there simply were not enough tires. If one could not travel, one was forced to stay home more. In the end, it was perhaps the local businesses in town—which played up the fact that one did not need to drive anywhere to buy a gift for Mother's Day or a loaf of bread—that benefited the most in the long run from tire rationing.

By mid-1942, the tire shortage was compounded by gas production being shifted toward military usage, with local citizens once again feeling the pinch. "What? No gas?" Or: "Watcha tryin' to give me? What do you mean no gas?" Or: "What? I have a ration card, what do you mean?—give me some gas!" And "Please, mister, I've got to get to work tonight—it means my job!" All those and more were answered in flat, cold words at the Denville gas stations: "Sorry, we're all out. Don't know for sure when we'll get any more." One service station operator reported several women breaking down in tears when told there was no gas, and another man offering to pay four times the amount for a single gallon.[102] Those who had once complained that their basic "A" designation and ration book entitled them to only 102 gallons of gas for a year's use looked back fondly to the time when they were even able to fill up their tanks. The shortages at the pumps in Morris County were more common toward the end of each month, before the service stations were resupplied at the beginning for a new month. Still, the gas shortage disrupted more than just passenger vehicles. At the beginning of 1943, the Denville dairies were hit hard by the rations. Local businesses warned the townsfolk that milk deliveries in town might have to end. Albert Doramun of the Diamond Spring Dairy, who had been driving 1,500 miles a month to cover his route, was allowed 78 gallons for three months. He was forced to move his delivery to every other day and sometimes even twice a week.[103] The remaining dairies in the vicinity were forced to do the same.

The Denville Garage on Main Street, circa 1944. *Denville Historical Society.*

Speaking of food; World War II had fundamentally changed the eating habits and diet of the people back home. The *Denville Herald* began running weekly columns titled "Your Home and Mine" and "Your Victory Garden," to provide some guidance and ease people into the new realities of life. Food was in short supply for various reasons: much of the processed and canned foods were reserved for shipping overseas to U.S. military forces and the Allies; transportation of fresh foods was limited due to gasoline and tire rationing and the priority of transporting soldiers and war supplies instead of food; imported foods, like coffee and sugar, were limited due to restrictions on importing.[104] Grocery shopping became quite a challenge during the conflict, as ration stamps more or less dictated the menus and recipes of home cooks. Some would skimp on many meals and hoard ration coupons to save them for special occasions, as one could not buy an item unless they had the ration stamp. Once the given stamps were used for the month, the person was no longer able to buy the product, regardless of whether they had the money for it or not. In examining newspapers from the time, food store advertisements reveal the lack of variety in available meat products, while restaurants in town touted their "victory" menus with delicacies that one could not ordinarily get in a store.

Denville became home to many nutrition groups and classes. Housewives were invited to come and learn how to make do with what they had available to them. Shared recipes often called for making food last a few days. Marie

War Ration Book, Gasoline Ration Card and Fuel Oil Stamp of a Denville resident from the time of war. These are now displayed at the Denville Museum. *Denville Historical Society*.

Doorman, a nutrition specialist of the Extension Service, New Jersey College of Agriculture, shared pointers at a nutrition meeting in town in February 1942. She said the secret was in varying the appearance of the same food that is served a second time. "For instance, meat loaf can be served at three dinners—hot the first time, cold the second, and as a base of chili can corn the third," she pointed out to the Denville women in attendance.[105] A Red Cross–run, ten-week nutrition course met on Wednesdays in the lecture room of the Denville School. "The course will cover practical training in conservation of food value, selection and preservation of food which will meet nutritional needs of you and your family," described Mrs. Westcott of Denville when asked what one might learn by taking the course. In April, another course taught women how to take advantage of the month's large egg supply in New Jersey and store eggs in jars for future consumption. In yet another course held in the Denville School later in the year, a demonstration agent outlined a week's full of meals that could be made from "thrifty" meat and canned food.

When it came to grocery shopping, one had to be frugal and smart about allocating stamps. Whether at a larger Safeway Food Store or the smaller

"Stretch Rationed Foods" Recipe Card on display at the Denville Museum. *Denville Historical Society.*

Dickerson's Market in town, customers would begin their food shopping armed with a ration book, a small notebook and a pencil. The notebook would contain a handy cutout of a "Daily Point Budget Record Chart" from the *Denville Herald*, which allowed the shopper to keep a record of their daily point expenditures and know every day how many points they

DAILY POINT BUDGET RECORD

DAY	RED STAMPS					BLUE STAMPS		
	MEAT	CHEESE	BUTTER	COOKING FATS	CANNED FISH	CANNED	PACKAGED	FROZEN
MON.								
TUES.								
WED.								
THURS.								
FRI.								
SAT.								
SUN.								
TOTALS								

GRAND TOTAL RED [ ] **BLUE** [ ]

FOR WEEK ENDING 194

Keep a record of your daily point expenditures, on this handy little chart which we have planned for your convenience. Know every day how many points you have left for each day's purchases; know always how many points you have left.

Read and Buy | THE HERALD | For More Profit

Daily Point Budget Record created by the *Herald* for shopping convenience when using rationing coupons. *From the* Denville Herald, *May 20, 1943.*

had left for each day's purchases.[106] On their mind was the countless advice from newspaper columns, such as one titled, "How to Buy Meat." "Don't hold out for your favorite cuts as there may not be enough of them to go around. There are more than 250 retail cuts of beef, pork, lamb, veal, and their by-products, and they all have approximately the same food value, and that's what counts."[107] There was also a massive variety of canned food, and not just fruits and vegetables. As reported in 1943, the already available for purchase, "365 items of canned food had added a new member to their increasing family—ham and eggs, America's favorite breakfast duet."[108] Of course, if fresh vegetables were available, they always won against their canned competition at the grocery store. Once home, all the stamp math added up to "victory meals." Harold Buchanan recalled many years later sitting in his home kitchen in Indian Lake. "My mom would buy margarine that was white and more like lard, and then you had to mix this yellow pill with it to make it look like butter." He would look at his mother and say, "Mom, this is not butter, where is the butter?"[109] Another Denville resident recalled another hack. "My mom would collect all the cooking grease and fat and then re-use it; sometimes she would give some to our neighbor to cook their meals in." And once it was time to do the dishes, "we would put remnants of old soap bars into a jar with some water and then use the slimy concoction to wash the dishes."[110] As an old adage says, "Waste not, want not."

Of course, if one could afford it, one could always go out for dinner at one of the restaurants in or around town. "Take Your Family Out to Dinner at the Boonton Victory Restaurant!" screamed one large advertising headline. Another, this time for Denville's famous Fireside Tavern in the center of town, announced, "Bring Your First Lady to Denville's FIRST Eating Place.…She'll be flattered by your good taste in bringing her here for our choice of food and intimate entertainment."[111] The ad also boasted the restaurant having three Chinese chefs for the most authentic "Oriental" as well as American cuisine. There was always the premier diner destination in town, namely, the Wayside Inn on Main Street. The famous hotel resort, restaurant and cocktail lounge offered dinner service throughout the war. Yet it was most known during the war for its yearly Thanksgiving dinner. On that date in November, servicemen ate free of charge and all others had a choice of a meal for every price point they could afford. Alvina Baggot, who was a teenager during the war, remembered always hanging out on the steps of the old restaurant. "The bartender there used to call us the 'Sad Sacks' because we would always hang out there in our military garbs." She remembered the ownership and staff being very friendly. "You would not know the war was going on. My girlfriend would go into the bar and put a nickel in the nickelodeon machine; we would then sit outside and listen to the music. They never chased us out, but even opened a window for us to hear it better, since we were too young to be permitted to stay inside."[112]

The most popular civilian war effort on the homefront was "Victory gardens." One saw such a garden everywhere one looked, in backyards, rooftops and even gas stations. In 1943 alone, Americans planted 20.5 million Victory gardens, which produced at least a third of all the vegetables eaten in the United States that year.[113] The *Herald* once more dedicated an entire page of its paper to a new weekly column, "Your Victory Garden," to which one could turn for hints and pointers about growing a garden. "If you have really hooked your heart to victory in the deepest sense of the word, you will receive a real thrill of accomplishment as you pick and carry your 'victory garden' vegetables to the kitchen for preparation," proclaimed Eliza M. Stephenson, the home services director for Denville.[114] The township fell in line behind the new initiative, naming a Victory garden chairman, organizing cooperative buying of seeds and fertilizer and getting plowing done for those who needed assistance. Soon after being appointed to the top position, Reverend Fletcher S. Gariss instructed students of Denville School to distribute official Victory garden pamphlet guides around town.[115] "For the new gardener, some advice…is always necessary. There is an old saying, that the successful farmer is one who can make two blades of grass grow where one grew before," announced the reverend at a PTA meeting at the Denville School. By means of newspaper articles and his pamphlet with basic hints and advice, the people of the town would learn how to be efficient "farmers."[116] As the citizens cared for their gardens, they did not tax the agricultural community already in need of assistance and at the same time were able to maintain their own sustenance.

Prewar years at a Denville produce store. It is a big difference from the rationing days that followed. By 1944, most of the produce was grown in local Victory gardens. *Denville Historical Society.*

While most people acted accordingly in the face of restrictions and rationing, there were some who would go above the law in search of profit. The "black market" did not escape the small lakeside town of Denville. It made available most goods for purchase without a stamp, even though one had to pay for them with higher prices. Subsequently, hijacking of rationed products, as well as the stamps themselves, became quite common. Gearhart's Service Station on Route 6 in Denville found itself a victim of two separate burglaries in the month of August 1944. The first time, two truck tires, gasoline coupons, gas in jerry cans and cash were taken. On the second occasion, the thieves took ten out of twenty-one tires, two dollars in bills but no coins and a delivery truck.[117] The truck was later found without its wheels and tires and with the gas tank emptied. Back in 1942, Robert W. Kratz had walked out of the Wayside Inn after enjoying a lunch with his wife, only to see his coworker from nearby Picatinny Arsenal shutting the door to Robert's car and quickly walking away. "I yelled at him to stop and demanded for him to give back what he took out of my glove compartment. I knew what he had taken." Frank Mezzino indeed did steal from his friend, tearing out two sheets of coupons from Kratz's ration book that the latter kept in his car. "He handed them back to me when I demanded them and when I asked him why, he said he wanted to make a trip to New York and didn't want to use his own coupons."[118] Despite returning the stolen stamps, Mezzino was questioned by the police and asked to appear before the town's magistrate. The case was followed by officials all over the gas-rationed East, as it was the first involving the theft of ration coupons, reported the *Denville Herald* a month later.[119]

Not long after the event in Denville, the OPA issued an order requiring all motorists to write on the front of all gasoline ration stamps their present motor vehicle license number and state of registration. Any stamps not endorsed in this manner would be invalid. The OPA district director pointed out that the changes were part of a new intensive drive against the gasoline black market in northern New Jersey.[120] Under the new program, distributors and retailers were held responsible for any invalid coupons they accepted. It is interesting that the impetus for combating the gasoline black market was at least partly a result of an incident in a small town in New Jersey. As a side note, while many people thought that Mezzino's punishment was going to be mandatory jail time, the Denville prosecutor did not even let the case go to trial. He simply fined the man nine dollars. Perhaps it was hard to confine a man to jail for doing something so many others were doing and not getting caught for: chiseling, swindling and hoarding their way through rationing.

Chapter 4

DRIVES, DRIVES
AND MORE DRIVES

L iving with shortages and rationing was not the end goal of the civilian effort; in a sense, it was just the beginning. While many people tightened their belts, the government still needed more of their help, this time with financing the war, conserving valued war material and helping fill war-industry jobs. Denville was once again on the front lines of the new efforts. As the U.S. Treasury and the Federal Reserve set off to raise war funds through heavier taxation and domestic borrowing through bond drives, the small town stepped up to the plate to do its part. "America is calling for assistance and sacrifice from every child in America to help keep our Freedom. After much thinking…[there are two] worthy causes, namely: first, raising the purchase of Defense Stamps in Denville. Second, supplying tin cans, rubber, newspapers, etc., essentials which Uncle Sam needs badly to help Defense Production," said Emily Sammon, a forty-year-old housewife of Denville in 1942. Adding to the federal large-scale bond drives were more local initiatives. Fiscal efforts of small-town America to help finance the war effort included supplementary scrap drives, the township war fund and even the Morris County War Chest collection, together with Red Cross monetary quotas. The U.S. bill for waging war was massive. In 2020 dollars, World War II cost the nation $4.1 trillion, according to data from the Congressional Research Service.[121] This is in comparison to the $1.5 trillion spent on America's longest conflict, the war in Afghanistan, plus the anti-terror campaigns in Iraq and Syria.[122] Needless to say, the people of Denville went to work collecting scrap, buying war bonds, filling war jobs and raising money for local collections and drives.

Reverend Wallace G. Sorenson, minister of the Community Methodist Church, was chosen chairman of the Denville Salvage Committee by the Local Defense Council. His duty was to arrange for and then supervise the town's collection of wastepaper, old metal, rubber and other valuable materials. "Bomb 'em with Junk!" proclaimed the first advertising campaign of the committee.[123] People were informed that 50 percent of every tank, ship and gun was made from scrap iron and steel. Other metals, rubber, rags, manila rope and burlap bags were also needed for making bombs, fuses, binoculars, planes, tires for Jeeps, gas masks barrage balloons, wiping rags for guns, parachutes and flares. Even waste cooking fats, wastepaper and tin cans did not escape the call to war. "Saving 'Scrap' Is Everyone's Job!" stated yet another local advertisement.[124] The editor of the *Denville Herald* added, "Collections in this country are not in it with the Nazis for efficiency and thoroughness. We rely on good will and patriotism where they give orders… let's show them that patriotism can do as well and better than compulsion."[125] The salvage drive in Denville began in earnest in September 1942. Salvage items were placed on the curb in front of each house on Saturday mornings throughout the month, and township trucks came around to collect them. Apart from the weekend pickups, a central depot was established near the post office on Broadway where one could bring scrap. Before the Scouts and local children were employed in the collection of scrap—which became the norm as the war went on—the central depot in the center of town began to resemble what the locals called a "mountain of junk."[126] According to committeeman and eventual town mayor John F. Hogan, the Broadway depot held over two hundred tons of scrap. "It is quite a sight, the mass is piled up almost to the height of the buildings on either side and with only a narrow passage alongside Armbruster's [Jewelry store next door]," he stated when asked about the town's response to the first scrap drive. "Beds seemed to have made up the largest single reservoir of old metal, and the balance is an assortment of old auto fenders and parts, kitchenware, wire, some tin cans, a few old drums, and empty artillery shell and other pieces whose original use can only be guessed," Hogan added with a chuckle. The nation called for scrap, and Denville answered.

Before they were officially called upon to help, either as Boy Scouts or Girl Scouts, young adults and kids saw scrap drives as a means of doing their part to help win the war. "Stop any High School Student and he will pick up anything you have!" advertised the *Herald*; it was not a wrong assumption.[127] The model of the children's enthusiasm originated with kids much younger than high school students. In late September 1942, near "Lashtown," the intersection of Morris Avenue and Savage Road in Denville, sprouted a noble pile of junk collected by children. Robert Casey, four-year-old son of Mr. and Mrs. Matthew Casey of George Street, and George Herzog, six, of George Street, did most of the work with their express wagons.[128] From the barn of the town's building inspector, George Lash, and from other houses and buildings in the neighborhood came old beds, springs, a scoop and various other metal articles. Prominent on the pile were several of the children's outgrown bicycles. "The whole thing started when the youngsters overheard us speaking to George Lash about the coming scrap collection. They got busy right away and soon had a fine heap ready for the township truck," stated one of the kids' parents.[129] Al Sippel, a Denville resident who was a young teen when the war started—and only three years away from partaking in the D-Day invasion in Normandy, France—recalled nearly eighty years later how he would spend his free time collecting scrap on weekends. "The owner of the Brennen Shoe Store right on Broadway had a [car] with a rumble seat, and he used to pick up kids in town and drive them around Indian Lake and Rainbow Lake collecting aluminum. We would go around knocking on people's doors collecting old pots and pans."[130]

As the war progressed, children began to organize at the Denville School. Pupils of the fifth and sixth grades formed a club called the "Defense Guards," with the goal of encouraging the purchase of War Savings Stamps, collecting scrap and doing all that was possible for the good of the country. The upper grades, namely seventh, eighth and ninth, added to the Defense Guards a subsection called the "Rifle Club." The marksmen used their own ammunition, purchased with funds raised through donations, with the biggest coming from the Picatinny Arsenal in Dover.[131] By mid-1943, the school reported having gathered sixty bushels of processed tin cans, which was then sent away for recovery of the tin.[132] "Helping Uncle Sam is the theme of our Denville School," said Principal Davenport at one of the school assemblies, emphasizing salvage campaigns for recovery of tin cans, waste fats and nylon hoses—the last spearheaded by the local Girl Scout troop.[133] Speaking of Scouts, through their efforts, Denville was able to contribute greatly to the war industry's need for scrap paper. Beginning in 1942, Boy Scouts Troop 17 of Indian Lake spent nearly every Saturday morning collecting old newspapers and magazines, which were then picked up by township trucks. After collecting about eighteen tons of paper within a five-month period in that first year, the troop donated 50 percent of its cash returns to local organizations. The council voted to give ten dollars to the Denville Ambulance Fund, sixteen dollars to the Red

Flag-raising for season reopening of Indian Lake beach, 1943. *Denville Historical Society*.

Cross for the purchase of supplies for use at the casualty stations and ten dollars to the Community Church.[134]

Paper drives as well as tin scrap drives became the pride and joy of the town's youngsters. Speaking at the local Defense Council meeting, the guest speaker, Director William A. Wachenfeld of the State Civilian Defense, praised the town for its efforts to maintain and increase collections, allowing the maintenance of the schedule of war production at the Sewaren and Carteret plants in New Jersey, where most of Denville's scrap shipments were sent.[135] Denville was indeed ahead of the game when it came to its "scrapping." In a letter to the public published in January 1945, the newly appointed chairman of the Denville Salvage Committee, John F. Hogan—Reverend Sorenson had resigned the post in anticipation of going into service—congratulated the people of the small town on their salvage record for 1944. "76 tons 750 lbs. of wastepaper was collected in Denville Township through your local Defense Council by Township Trucks. Seven tons of tin cans were collected by our school children and our citizens who placed tin cans in the container in at the Post Office." He then christened the first Sunday of each month a "Wastepaper Day in Denville."[136] Even the local businesses chipped in to the war effort and followed the youngsters' lead. None was more active than the recently constructed Denville Theatre in the center of town.

"Flash! Flash! Boys and Girls Under 12 Years of Age; Help Win the War Now! Bring 25 Pounds of Wastepaper to the Denville Theatre and Be Admitted FREE on THURSDAY."[137] The movie theater, built in 1937, was the town's main hub and attraction. It was where people of all ages went to catch a movie, get some news from the front or simply hang out with friends and family. The movies played every day of the week at 2:00, 7:00 and 9:00 p.m., with informational and defense movies for air wardens and the Denville Defense Committee members scheduled in between. More importantly, the theater, together with the post office, played a pivotal role in various local drives. When asked about the role of the local business, Harry V. Gable, a Morris County sheriff, stated in 1942, "On the occasion of the 5th anniversary of the Denville Theatre the management is celebrating by providing another service to the country in addition to furnishing wholesome amusement to the public, thereby keeping up morale. They are now selling war stamps to help stamp out the murderous dictator Hitler of Germany and the miserable [sic] dogs who stabbed our boys in the back at Pearl Harbor."[138] It was in fact at the theater that the first war stamp was sold in Denville. In another war fundraiser, children were admitted to

Flash! Flash!
BOYS and GIRLS
(UNDER TWELVE YEARS OF AGE)
Help Win The War Now!

Bring 25 Pounds of Waste Paper
To The DENVILLE THEATRE
And Be Admitted FREE
ON THURSDAY
Matinee Only, August 17th

See "BETWEEN TWO WORLDS"
with John Garfield
As An Added Attraction You Will See
"MY FRIEND FLICKA"
with Roddy McDowall

All persons between 12 and 16 years of age will be admitted for half price upon bringing 25 lbs. of paper or more. NOTE: - Paper will be received in the lobby of the theatre from 1 p.m. to 3 p.m. The show will start at 2 p.m.

JOHN F. HOGAN,
Chairman
Salvage Committee
Denville Township

Above: The Denville Theatre as it was being constructed in the 1930s. *Denville Historical Society*.

Left: The Denville Theatre ad from wartime. *From the Denville Herald*.

This picture, recently discovered in the files of the Denville Historical Society, shows the chairman of the Denville Salvage Committee, John F. Hogan (*right*), symbolically receiving paper salvage in front of the Denville Theatre in the center of town. *Denville Historical Society.*

a matinee show by bringing in canned food and/or tin cans. But perhaps the most bizarre campaign took place in the latter years of the war, when patrons lined up by the theater's entrance to sign…a bomb. Courtesy of the state administrator and Picatinny Arsenal, every bond purchaser had "the pleasure of writing their name on [the bomb], at which time [it] will be loaded and sent overseas to bring victory nearer."[139] When asked about the event, the owner added, "Who knows, maybe your son or relative will fire this same bomb…and every Bond Purchaser will see the show free with their bonds waiting for them when they leave!"[140]

Through the duration of the war, Americans purchased over $156 billion in war bonds, which accounted for nearly half of the government's war spending.[141] While the seven full national bond drives were a constant presence in small-town America, they were supplemented through local monetary drives, which had as much of an impact on the wallets of local citizens. One knew when a new bond drive came around; you simply couldn't miss it. The *Denville Herald* even sacrificed its own weekly paper by writing in big letters across all the pages—and thus covering the stories within—"BUY WAR BONDS!"[142] Posters and advertisements with official U.S. Treasury War Bond quotas for New Jersey were plastered all over the post office and local papers, reminding everyone to do their part. The New Jersey poster even had a map of the state broken into different counties with specific quotas requested for each one. Each drive came with ads informing the public of what their bond really "purchased." These included infographics about bridges, tanks, uniforms and bombs and usually ended with something like, "If you and every American invests at least 10 percent of your income in War Bonds every pay day we can supply our fighting forces with these essentials to a victorious war."[143] Newspapers also managed to slip in small messages between articles along the lines of how not buying bonds was equal to aiding the enemy. Some people needed that extra push, and that is where the "minute men" came in.

"Minute Men to Visit Every Home in Denville in U.S. War Bond Drive!" announced a headline in August 1942. That week, all families found themselves opening the door to young men with pledge books.[144] One could refuse but seldom did. The volunteers were dubbed "Minute Men," and their base of operations was the Denville Community Church. They made their way around town each day and night, fulfilling their promise of "reaching every family." In fact, "if early reports are indicative of results, the Denville Minute Man March…showed close to a 100 percent coverage desired, with a total of 500 pledges to purchase war bonds as rapidly as the buyers' incomes would permit," stated Alfred L. Huelsenbeck, general chairman of the drive.[145] For a town that had between 3,600 and 4,400 people—based on various estimates at the time—and if we account for the fact that pledges came not from youngsters and nonworking elderly but from families, the number of pledges seems quite significant.

As they did with scrap drives, local Scouts and school-age children also got behind soliciting pledges and selling war bonds. Troop 17 of Indian Lake and Troop 67 of St. Mary's Church were even more successful than the official Minute Men, as they secured $1,950 in pledges in just one week in 1944.[146] This time, it was someone you knew when that doorbell rang instead of a county volunteer, and that made the difference. Still, residents were reminded "to receive the call of the Boy Scout bond salesman in a friendly manner, recognizing that he is performing a patriotic act."[147] And for those still hesitant, the caption "So You Can't Buy Another Bond?"

The War Bond Drive took over the entire issue of the *Denville Herald* with large lettering on every page of the 1942 issue. *From the* Denville Herald, *August 20, 1942.*

appeared under the picture of a dead and badly mutilated G.I. on the front page of the paper, giving them that extra push. The notice, published by the U.S. Treasury, also included the following text: "Take a good look at this American soldier...victim of a Jap raid. It is not a pleasant scene is it? When you are asked to buy an extra War Bond...think of this picture of your fellow American blasted by the concussion of a Jap bomb thousands of cities from home." The somber ad finished with, "Then brother, don't you think you will want to dig a little deeper to back up his comrades?"[148] A scan of the numbers of bond pledges and purchases in Denville shows that the war bond campaign worked. In fact, for some, it worked really well. By November 1944, numerous newspapers reported that Denville Township was credited with at least two $1,000 bonds sold in the Sixth War Loan, something of a feat, as the bond denominations started with the most popular bond of $25. The famous bonds were purchased by the owner of the Safeway Food Store and the owner of the Denville Shack Restaurant.[149]

Selling bonds to the average American not only held inflation at bay but also tied the interests of the American people to that of the government. According to the Museum of American Finance, bonds not only redirected the demand from consumer goods but also, more importantly, decreased the likelihood of civil unrest by making the government a debtor to as many people as possible. As bondholders disdain anything that threatens the security of their principal interest—from Hitler down to their neighbor trying to cheat the ration system—it was in everyone's interest to support the government and its war effort.[150] The problem lay in the fact that low-wage workers, the poor, the elderly and the young seldom had enough money to afford the lowest bond denomination of $25.00. In 1942, production workers averaged only $0.86 per hour, which rose to only about $1.06 by the war's end.[151] That is where stamp books came into play. For a little spare change of $0.25, people could purchase a war stamp, sold at the Denville Post Office, the Denville Theatre or Gardner's Gift Shoppe. This was a bargain, as once the book was filled with seventy-five stamps, the owner could trade it in for a $25.00 bond. That was a discount, as doing so would equate to an expenditure of short of $19.00. In Denville, as in many areas around the nation, the sale and purchase of war stamps was directed at the young. Namely, it became one of the main initiatives of the "School at War" program that was organized directly after Pearl Harbor and sponsored by the War Savings Staff of the Treasury Department in conjunction with the U.S. Office of Education. It strongly encouraged the purchase and sale of War Saving Stamps. Winning schools were offered incentives at the end of each year that ranged from trophies to sponsored school trips to national monuments.

As much pressure as existed for the adult population to contribute, the youth of the small town also felt the societal push to spend their—or their parents'—money. The *Denville Herald* posted monetary totals from the Denville School and the Union Hill School per teacher's name and home room; those not pulling their weight were put on the spot. The *Herald* was quick to point out a dip in stamp buying during 1943's Christmas

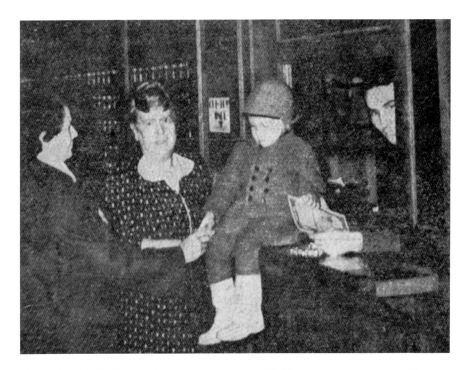

Mrs. Arthur Hopler brought her youngest son, Lowell J. Hopler, down to the post office to buy a fifty-dollar Defense Bond, circa 1942 *Denville Historical Society.*

break, when "gift buying interfered somewhat with purchases of War Saving Stamps at the Denville School."[152] Things picked up in the coming months; by April, it was reported that the school was able to buy $760 worth of stamps in March, bringing the school total to a staggering $4,000 to that point in 1943. This time, the biggest contribution came from the sixth-grade classroom, outpacing the fourth grade from the month prior.[153] The student's ability to continue to make strides in their purchasing power was attributed to part-time and summer jobs. While the pupils purchased $148 worth of stamps and bonds in September 1942, in that same month in 1943, they bought more than $700 worth, a 400 percent increase. It was not just the buying but also the selling of stamps that propelled Denville and the Morris County schools into statewide recognition. By July 1945, shortly before the conclusion of World War II, it was reported that the schools of Morris County had sold and/or purchased nearly $2 million worth of stamps and bonds since the inception of the "Schools at War" program following December 7, 1941. The sales in the schools in 1945 alone amounted to $650,000.[154]

The amount of bonds and stamps sold in Denville seem that much more significant when one considers all the additional charitable organizations that vied for the citizens' hearts and pockets. Created within months of America's entry into the war, a new project was organized, the Morris County War Chest. It "combined the many worthwhile local, national and international charities into one big War Chest, rather than attempt a large number of smaller drives which would consume time, gasoline and tires, that [were] so urgently needed in other war activities."[155] The Morris County War Chest became the prime organization collecting money from the townsfolk, concurrent with and during the breaks from the bigger national bond drives. Among the better-known members of the more than thirty organizations that looked to it for funds were the United Service Organization, the Navy Relief Society and the various National War Relief Societies, such as the British, Polish and French. The goal for the Morris County War Chest in 1942, the first year of its existence—and before it more than tripled by the last year of the war—was to raise $265,000. When it was reported that Denville fell just short of its goal of $2,000 in the Morris County War Chest, the advertising machine cranked up the pressure.[156] A full-page ad with a starving, skeleton-like child holding an empty bowl asked, "How Big Is Your Heart?"[157] William H. Mason Jr., the general campaign chairman of the Morris County War Chest, spoke at the following year's kickoff. "The War Chest offers [the people of Morris County] the ability to work on three fronts; military front, since some of its agencies serve our armed forces; the Allied Nations front, where the contributions prove to the people of the countries fighting with us that [we are with them]; and the home front, where the contributions insure the continued operation of organizations working here in our country and serving our needs [such as hospitals]."[158] Together with various proclamations and pleas by the mayor and the editor of the *Herald*, the ad campaign once again did the trick. Denville not only met, but also then surpassed by 50 percent, the Morris County War Chest quota for 1943.

If Americans had any money or time left, the Red Cross beckoned them to give more of each. The scope of the organization's contribution to the war effort exceeds the space dedicated here. Yet, it needs to be noted that the Red Cross worked as much back home as it did at the front in helping those touched by the conflict. At home, millions of volunteers provided comfort and aid to members of the armed forces and their families, served hospitals suffering from severe shortages of medical staff, produced emergency supplies for war victims and maintained training programs in home nutrition and first

Morris County sheriff Harry Gable (*right*) bought the first War Savings Stamp at the opening of the Denville Theatre's fifth-anniversary celebration. *From the* Denville Herald, *July 30, 1942.*

aid.[159] As it was mostly a volunteer organization, its reach for help extended into small-town America as much as any other monetary relief funds. Mrs. William Kellett of Union Hill took it upon herself to host Red Cross sewing meetings at her home throughout the conflict. She and her friends sewed sweaters, shirts and socks for soldiers, all according to Red Cross guidelines. Another citizen, Mrs. John Hogan, extended her work beyond the Red Cross by volunteering to make clothes for those who had recently enlisted or were drafted from Denville, to be directly shipped to them by their loved ones back home. "I handknitted sweaters and sent them to eight Denville boys in the Army and Navy, and I am making eight more." She then added, "Names of 16 more in the armed forces were given to me with the measurements for sweaters; if any more parents would like sweaters for their sons [and want to send them directly instead of going through the Red Cross], they can notify me." Within a few short months, dedicated sewing rooms were created at the Denville Community Church and St. Mary's Church, as well the Public Library and the Denville School. All sewing machines were donated by local citizens. In July 1945, the various Red Cross groups in town were able to complete 59,880 surgical dressings in one month. The feat was nothing short of spectacular; when the Red Cross Surgical Dressing Units started up in Denville, their output was measured in the tens, not thousands.

Apart from making goods for the fighting men through the Red Cross and through personal initiatives—as was the case with Mrs. Hogan—the town welcomed instructors of first-aid courses that were offered almost continuously between 1942 and 1945. The courses offered at the Denville Community Church and at the Denville School attempted to fill in for the shortage of nurses in the area. The courses usually consisted of ten two-hour lessons in which young women would learn how to care for the sick and the wounded. One of the courses in February 1942 that took place in Denville addressed the specific need for "home nurses." E.J. Ebans, director of first aid and public health for the Local Defense Council, stated, "The shortage of the nurses in this vicinity makes it necessary to get as many women as possible qualified to care for invalids."[160] The response to the Red Cross home nursing course was so great that, it was reported, new sections had to be made available. Of course, besides volunteering for nursing courses and eventually aid stations, people could also donate, and this time it was not just money. When the Mobile Red Cross Blood Bank visited the area in July 1942, it departed with 107 pints of blood.[161] Special recognition was given to people who contributed a gallon of their blood to the armed forces through the Red Cross. They were granted rewards at various intervals, beginning with ribbons and ending with a silver emblem for the final donation. As reported by the *Denville Herald*, at least one person from Denville qualified for the membership in the Donor Gallon Club by the summer of 1944.[162]

Finally, Denville citizens and organizations held events to raise funds for the Red Cross. In between trying to raise money for a Jeep, and even a partaking in the "Buy a Bomber" campaign of April 1943, the townsfolk took it on themselves to assist one of the most revered humanitarian organizations in the world. The Rockaway River Country Club in Denville held seasonal benefit dances for the American Red Cross War Relief Fund, and the Wayside Inn hosted the annual Spring Fashion Show and Dance Party, with all proceeds going to the Red Cross Fund. The latter event was a whole town affair, as the premier restaurant in town donated its space, the Broadway clothing stores donated the clothes and fashions and the local beauty salons offered their services to the models, all local young women. Perhaps the most heartwarming Red Cross fundraising story was told by Fred S. Canre, the chairman of the Denville Branch of the American Red Cross, which, in September 1942, received a three dollar donation from the most unlikely source, seven-year-old Lucile Fisher of Lake Arrowhead Community. "[The young lady and her friends] decided they would put on a show for the benefit of the Red Cross in front of their home for any young visitors that dropped in. They all did something, either singing, dancing, reciting, or maybe just pulling the curtain back and forth or taking up admissions, which they set at 5 cents. While the audience, mostly composed of mothers of the group, brought the box office receipts up to somewhere around a dollar, when the word began to spread and fathers and neighbors began to chip in, it quickly rose to $3." The chairman was so touched by the story that he decided to spread the news of it whenever he could. "If a bunch of kids can do that for the Red Cross, what couldn't grownups do if they tried?" he added.[163] And so, with all the various drives raising money, whether national or local in scope, Denville's townsfolk never wavered in their commitment to helping the war effort, no matter how small the donation nor how small the person making the donation.

THE STORY OF DONATING massive amounts of money to the war cause isn't complete without a note on the quickly changing nature of work, jobs and labor during the great conflict. According to the Industrial Department of New Jersey Power & Light Company from 1945, more than three dozen vital products needed by the armed forces to speed victory over the Axis powers were manufactured in the west Morris County area, including Dover, Rockaway, Denville, Netcong and Stanhope.[164] The report pointed out the important roles played in the area by employees and industrial plants, as well as farmers and others working in war industries. It also, albeit indirectly, showed the changes in work habits and norms for those living in the area. Subsequently, the information brings to light the assumption of how more job opportunities might have led to slightly more wealth and people's ability to "give" to the war effort. The jobs were indeed plentiful, considering that just a few years earlier Denville and the nation were still in the midst of the Great Depression. From the large war plants in the area—Picatinny Arsenal in Dover being the main one, employing as many as eighteen thousand people—to the small machine shops that turned out precision equipment, war materials poured out from the area to the fighting fronts between 1942 and 1945.[165]

Some of the products manufactured locally included artillery fuses, box manufacturing machinery and steel, iron and brass castings. Farmers made agricultural products, cattle feed and milk products and raised grains, meat and truck-farm vegetables. Men and women manufactured concrete blocks and pipes, crushed stone, construction materials and drilling machinery, dynamite, forgings and hoses for gasoline and oil. Other products included incendiary bombs, flares, iron and zinc ore and many more, including vital ordnance material for the army and the navy.[166] The U.S. Employment Service Office hung posters in the Denville Post Office, Gardner's Gift Shoppe and Lysaght's Liquor Store advertising "Part-Time Employment Opportunity—Vital Work."[167] Advertising transportation provided to and from work, the notice invited sixteen-year-old or older boys to "contribute to the war effort by accepting part-time employment in an establishment near [their] home." Interestingly, those asked to apply had to be "130 pounds in weight and be physically able to perform laboring work." In fact, scanning through the classified section of the *Denville Herald*, one can see the different job opportunities available to local citizens. The jobs included mechanic helpers, welders, construction laborers and chemists in Boonton's E.F. Drew Chemical Plant. Wright's Aeronautical Corporation claimed to have "200 Special Machine Shop War Jobs set aside [for young men]."[168]

There was also the Picatinny Arsenal in next-door Dover, which at the time was the country's principal source of research on artillery ammunition and one of the biggest producers of arms. Accordingly, the personnel increased from nearly 2,000 to 18,000 workers during the duration of the war to meet the demand. Ads in Denville began popping up for room rentals for Picatinny workers moving into the area. This was more than encouraged by the plant when it "appealed to householders in Denville and vicinity to list with their Special Service Office any rooms they may have available."[169] The *Herald* joined the cause with its half-page editorial revealing that hardly a day went by without one or more people calling its office to see if the newspaper staff could tell them where they could rent a furnished room. "These people are working at the 'Arsenal' and are in dire need of a clean place to sleep—if they are to continue producing the arms and ammunition our country now needs so urgently."[170] The editor asked the townsfolk if they had a spare room or could double up. Thus, jobs influenced the small town beyond simple employment. That is not to say that Denville did not have people working at Picatinny. While exact numbers of locals employed by the plant is not available, we do know that three Denville men—out of thirteen chosen employees at the Picatinny Arsenal—received cash awards at the end of the war for "making time, labor and money saving suggestions, and improving the manufacturing process."[171] Christian M. McVey of Indian Lake received $250 for pointing out a way to modify punches used in assembling fuse components. Harry R. Stulit won $45 for submitting a suggestion to substitute paint for glass reflectors in building signs. Charles A. Riker's contribution is lost to history, but he was awarded $25 by the plant.

Other jobs in war-related industries employed Denville citizens in and around town. Athena Leonard, who was a student at the Denville School during the war, remembered her father working as a security guard at the Boonton airport (today it serves as a soccer field complex). "My dad worked at Aircraft Radio Field in Boonton during the war....He was a guard there. He walked around and patrolled the whole perimeter during the war. The military equipment used on Doolittle's and other war aircraft bombers was manufactured there."[172] What Athena's dad was protecting was the production headquarters of the Aircraft Radio Corporation's radio equipment for military aircraft. The corporation-designed equipment was installed in the first fighter squadrons of the U.S. Army Air Corps and the U.S. Navy; the company also designed and manufactured a great number of radios for World War II aircraft.[173]

Recalling her time in the war in a 2020 interview, ninety-five-year-young Elizabeth Hardy, a lifelong resident of Denville, recalled her time in the war.

I grew up running back and forth on Franklin Road which was a dirt road at the time. When I graduated Boonton High School [one of the optional high schools for Denville residents] *in 1942, I was seventeen years old. By that time, I knew my husband-to-be and he went into the service. My parents both worked at Picatinny. I stayed in touch with my husband through V-Mail—he got sick when in California and was discharged in 1943. When he got back, we got married and got an apartment.*

We had to have coupons to buy everything. There was a big demand for women to work in war-related industries. I worked at a mine in Mine Hill. It was all secretarial work; time keeping, switchboard—I always wanted to go down in the mine but I never did get there [that was reserved for men]. *It was the Scrub Oaks Mine* [a major New Jersey iron mine in magnetite ore].

Claire and Henry
Patterson during wartime.
Courtesy of Mr. Patterson.

> *I also worked part time at the police station in town. We all had to be fingerprinted back then during the war. It was in case we got bombed so they would know who we were.*[174]

Elizabeth was around eighteen at the time. She was a married woman of a serviceman and a war-industry worker whose parents both worked in a munition plant—all at an age at which many young people today are still trying to decide what college they should pick in the fall.

Claire Zieger of Cedar Lake, who was just one year removed from high school in 1943 when this story takes place, recalled in her memoir many years later:

> *Pop stated working in Western Electric in Clifton, NJ* [about 18 miles away]. *The country was at war when we went there and they were looking for help. Pop told me and I applied for work and was accepted. I made a lot more money. I worked 6 nights a week and earned about $33, which was considered good at the time. I was a relay adjuster. One of the things*

produced in Western Electric was radios for the army, navy, etc. A relay is a very small piece of equipment with short blades and the spacing between had to be very accurate. That's what I did—spaced them. I did not like that work at all, but it was my contribution toward helping the war effort. To break the monotony, our section had a radio which helped a lot. Pop was in a different part of the plant. It was very big, old brick factory. I had a good friend with whom I worked; we met there. Her name was Sophie Zak. She would come home with us on Saturday and spend Sundays with us. Pop and I rode with Nellie Heysenger who lived in Rockaway.

One time Nellie and Pop were both on vacation and I traveled down to work via train to Paterson and then took the bus. Once of the workers in our dept. who lived in Paterson asked me what I was doing on the bus after work—12:30 AM. I told her I took the bus to the train in Paterson. She was so distressed about it that she said you are coming home with me and I will walk you to the station [a very lonely place in not a good neighborhood]. *I told her I didn't want her to do that and why should she put herself in an uncomfortable situation. She told me she had a big police dog, and no one would bother either of us. She did that for two weeks! She was a black girl and was taking care of her brother and sister. I invited her up to* [Cedar] *Lake and she came to visit once with her boyfriend. How fortunate I was to have her help me like that. I walked home from the train station in Denville to Cedar Lake.*[175]

Claire's story also brings up another important aspect of the war's effect on the people of Denville; namely, the changing societal roles of women. Labor shortages that resulted from the military's demand for manpower created an opening for thousands of women, many in normally exclusive male domains, to enter fields previously restricted to them. And as with all other aspects of war, the new national norm did not escape the women of the small Morris County town.

Chapter 5

WE CAN DO IT!

Women of World War II

O n the eve of World War II, women compromised nearly 25 percent of the American labor force; by 1944, at the peak of female wartime employment, that number had jumped to 36.[176] Similarly, while women had gone off to war plenty of times in the past—most recently as army nurses for the American Red Cross during World War I—more than 300,000 women volunteered for the armed forces during the new global conflict. In New Jersey, women joined all of the newly established armed services, such as WAC (Women's Army Corps), WAVES (Women's Reserve, U.S. Naval Reserve), SPARS (U.S. Coast Guard Women's Reserve), WASP (Women Airforce Service Pilots) and the U.S. Army Nurse Corps. A post commander at Fort Monmouth in New Jersey commended the contributions of women entering the workforce: "Our WACs are filling many important jobs on the post. They have replaced men in clerical and desk jobs. They are driving trucks and jeeps; they are working as hospital technicians and attendants.…We could use twice their present number if we could only get them."[177] At the same time, working women and those entering the armed forces were still subject to female stereotypes of running households. They were also targeted by advertisements pertaining to cooking, cleaning and shopping. The small town of Denville, New Jersey, offers a perfect microcosm of typical war experiences, this time, those of women.

Elise E. Whiton, the associate editor of the *Denville Herald*, shared the following story in July 1945.

*A nice young lady from a government office dropped in to ask would we
please print an appeal for typists and stenographers to go to Washington to
help out with the paperwork down there. Just for the fun of it, to hear what
she'd say; we told the young lady that employers generally expect to pay for
Help Wanted ads, instead of asking publishers to print them for free. She
handled that one pretty well; said she has a couple of brothers in service and
had herself given up better paying work to do this, which she considers more
essential and patriotic....She probably could have just said that she was
working for nothing for the government, just as she was asking us to do.[178]*

The young lady's case was not atypical of the time. Many women whose
husbands, brothers, fathers and sweethearts fought on the front saw it as their
patriotic duty to work. To many, it was also the means to support themselves
and their families. Dr. John Gauer, chairman of the Denville Local Defense
Council, send out a call for all women between eighteen and thirty-five "who
can be spared from their homes without the determent to their families to
register immediately at the nearest United States Employment Agency."[179]
Once registered, the women were referred to jobs in war production or
to training courses that would fit them for such work. While the call was
initially limited to women under thirty-five, it was eventually opened for
older women, as "typists, clerks, and stenographers [were] needed so badly
by the Government agencies, that they [were] urged to take civil service
exams instead of going into actual productive work."[180] That is not to say
that women were also not in demand by the corporate sector, even more so
now that it was guided by new government regulations. By April 1942, it
was predicted that 100,000 additional workers would be needed in the war
plants of northern New Jersey by the end of that year.[181]

By mid-1942, the First Aid and Denville Motor Corps had graduated
sixteen young ladies from the standard and advanced motor mechanics
training course and a similar number from their transportation and safety
course. Things were changing for women back home, and they were
changing quickly. Ads and proclamations such as "Women Must Work!"
and "Looking for Women for War Work!" seemed to appear everywhere.
The long-running *Parents* magazine in its February 1943 issue ran a special
report on "War Jobs for Mothers," an article that promised to "help [them]
decide where [their] duty lied." On one hand, the article flaunted the 1941
Lanham Act, which provided funds for daycare of young children whose
mothers were working in war-related industries. On the other hand, it
pointed out that "if a mother chooses to stay at home and devote herself to

creative homemaking and child-rearing, she is, in the best sense, [still] a war worker in the home."[182] The article further added, "We are fighting this war to preserve the health and welfare of the family; and whether our job is in the armed forces, in the munition factories, on the farm producing crops, or in the home caring for children, it is all essential to the war effort."[183]

The choice was indeed a difficult one for many, as the pressures to do their part and of raising children mounted. This could perhaps be best exemplified by the news from the front page of the *Herald* from April 1, 1943. "Local Woman Takes Over Gas Station Job." The article praised Denville's Mrs. Fred Zisa, who, "though a housewife and mother of two children, has stepped into the place left by her husband's brother Private First Class Zisa at his service station in nearby Paterson."[184] Just three inches to the right on the same page was the headline, "Woman Takes Her Own Life." The thirty-three-year-old wife of a local doctor committed suicide by hanging herself by a clothesline from a pipe in the cellar of her home on Valley Road in Denville. She left behind her husband and two sons, seven and six years old.[185] Unfortunately, this was not the only case of female suicide in town. Another woman, notified of her husband's death, locked herself in her home with all the gas jets turned on. She was found on her couch in her Manor Road home with the picture of her husband clenched closely to her chest.[186]

In the *Parents* magazine article, it was noted that the first applicant for the new WACs (Women's Army Corps) was a mother of an eight-year-old child. It is not known whether the article was trying to say that even mothers could join the newly available auxiliary armed forces or simply presenting a fact. Yet it does bring up the important reality of women joining the U.S. armed forces. "Have you a hidden talent?" was the message from the adjutant general of the U.S. Army recruiting station. "If you'd like to find out what your special aptitude is and put it to work to help win this war—take the opportunity the WAC offers you! Join the WAC and let Army experts help you discover the type of work you can do best," he added.[187] Some from Denville were just curious enough to find out; not only for the WACs, but also for the WAVES, the SPARs and the Nursing Corps.

Dorothy Feiser, working behind the counter at Gardner's Soda Shoppe in town, could hardly contain her happiness when interviewed by a local journalist. The twenty-four-year-old history teacher, who supplemented her salary by having taken on the summer job just a week prior to being interviewed, became one of the few hundred WACs from the East—and the first one from Denville—accepted out of several thousand applicants.

One of the first WACs from Denville and the eventual recruiter, Dorothy Feiser. *From the* Denville Herald, *July 30, 1942.*

"I think it is a wonderful opportunity for any girl, and I know it will be a new experience for me," she said.[188] Before she reported to the training camp at Des Moines, Iowa, she indeed had the right to be delighted. It was stated that "excellent officer material for the Women's Army Corps was to be found among two types of women—first the business type and professional woman, and second, the competent wife and mother who ran her household with dispatch and efficiency."[189] Dorothy was indeed perfect for the job, having graduated from a teachers college and working multiple jobs. "It wasn't easy; I had to go through four examinations, one mental, one physical, and two personal interviews before I was notified of being selected," she stated in the same interview. Another local girl, also named Dorothy (Apgar), and also a teacher, was granted two months' salary when she informed her school in Parsippany that she had been accepted to the Navy WAVES. When the call came, just as it did for the young men, the local women would not shy away from answering it.

Miss Feiser was not only the first Denville girl to join the WACs but also became the agency's main recruiting agent for the area when she returned to the small town a year after her recruitment in 1943. Promoted twice since joining the year before and now a second officer (the equivalent of first lieutenant), Dorothy returned to Denville to share her story and hopefully inspire other young women to follow in her footsteps. Speaking before groups in town as part of the June recruiting drive, her message was always the same. "The WAC now has 65,000 women enrolled and want to increase to 150,000, each member releasing a man for combat duty," she stated, adding, "Pay is the same as for men in the Army!"[190] Her teacher background helped her get established in the army, further justifying the armed forces' insistence on looking for young women with business or professional backgrounds. "My assignments since being commissioned have been being an instructor on the officer candidate faculty and supervising instruction at Fort Des Moines, Iowa." To be able to work in recruiting, Dorothy had to undergo an intensive recruiting course at the WAC Training Center at Fort Oglethorpe, Georgia. When her recruiting duty ended after thirty days in the summer of 1943, she once again departed Denville and returned to Des Moines, where she was assigned as the supervisor in the plans and training office. From there, for Feiser of Denville, the only way was up. After excelling at her new assignment, Dorothy was selected to attend the Assistant General School at Fort Washington, Maryland, where she took part in and graduated from an administrative course. On her return to Iowa, she was appointed chief of the U.S. Army Clerks and promoted to captain, a position she held until the end of the war.

Feiser's brief visit seemed to be a precursor to a much larger, all-state WAC recruiting campaign that November. "The Army had authorized the establishment of State WAC companies and urged each town to call for WAC recruits to make up a portion of the Army's casualties for the United Sates in the war, approximately 70,000," announced the Denville chairman of the campaign, Alvina Studer.[191] It was planned to enlist one WAC for each of New Jersey's army casualties, which by that time numbered 2,212. All enlisted women received their state's special shoulder patch, which also carried the distinctive insignia of the All-States Division. "The WACs will train you for photography, radio, mechanics, weather, food, or other special jobs. Many of these skills will prove valuable after the war in a career, or in running a home," the chairman stated. To drum up interest, the Denville Theatre got involved by showing WACs educational videos free of charge, and the town committee headed by Mrs. Studer sponsored an essay contest for any girl fourteen to eighteen years of age on the topic of the Women's Army Corps.[192] By May 1944, motion picture theaters launched National WAC Recruiting Week—which the Denville Theatre was also a part of—with theaters hosting recruiting officers to answer questions and/or sign up willing women. The WAC Recruiting Campaign even reached the annual Mother and Daughter Banquet at the Denville Community Church. A recruiting officer was the key speaker, a job usually reserved for Reverend Charles Mead of the local parish.[193]

Once again, the Denville ladies answered the call. Mr. and Mrs. Leonard Cobb of Franklin Road, Union Hill, Denville, became one of the few couples in the country—if there were any others—to have three daughters in the Women's Army Corps. Their daughters Harriet, Carol and Janet were convinced to enlist after the WAC Recruiting Week festivities in Denville. Soon, the small town was represented all over the world, with Ethel Samuels of Cedar Lake sending her parents pictures of her work with the armed forces in New Guinea. As part of a nursing unit, she also spent portions of her war years in China and Australia. In another letter from New Guinea,

Helen Mutz *(front row, second from right)* with her WAC unit. *Courtesy of Mr. Walter Mutz.*

this time to her friend, she described a typical life of a small-town girl as a nurse in the U.S. Army's Nurse Corps during World War II.

> *My assignment now is that of a day room specialist. I am building a 5-day rooms for the first WAC unit to arrive in New Guinea.*
>
> *I have my own little jeep and I bump along the roads all day. Our social life could be one continuous whirl but we are much too tired to get involved. The way the girls have adjusted themselves to this new life is something to marvel at. Bugs, snakes, and rats bother us not and we are beginning to reach the point where we think them cute.*
>
> *We have to wear G.I. clothes at all times and when we dress up it is no great task as all we have to do is put on a clean pair of G.I. pants*
>
> *I have traveled some 1,500 miles by plane since I reached New Guinea. Every day is more interesting than the day before. I have seen Jap prisoners and talked to women who were prisoners of the Japs. The great respect shown us by the G.I.'s is more than enough compensation for the fact that we are away from home. Every little thing we do is appreciated, whether it is a smile or a few words, or a cold drink.*[194]

Another young lady, WAC private Dorothy Hanlon, also found herself writing her parents back in Denville, this time from England. In her letter, she praised the American Red Cross's support that she witnessed in her time overseas. "The American Red Cross has given us so much since we left the States. Please do all you can for them at home. You have no idea the work they do for us. Someday I hope to make it known to everyone."[195] There were many young women from the area who joined the armed forces. When the Denville Theatre opened its doors to the WAC recruits, they did not know that they would shortly need to place a classified ad for a job opening, as young Veronica Fowler, the main casher, was herself persuaded to join the Women's Army Corps. Yet it was not just the WACs or the Army Nursing Corps that recruited the Denville girls. The other military branches also came calling.

While women joined the WACs, the Army Nursing Corps and the Red Cross more often than the other military agencies, there are a few known instances of Denville's young women looking for different military opportunities. As Barbara V. Jaeger of the Army Nursing Corps managed a hospital clinic for the Ninth Troop Carrier Pathfinders at an air base in France, her friend from back home, Anita D. Straus, decided to join the WAVES and was sent to the Pacific theater of the war. Marjorie H. Bublitz on the other hand chose the SPARs and stayed back stateside in New York with the U.S. Coast Guard, where she was in charge of the mailroom. Thus, while all three ladies joined the armed forces from the same small town, they wound up in different theaters of the conflict, from the Pacific, to Europe and, finally, the homefront. The younger ladies who were still too young to join read the *Denville Herald*'s weekly comic strip, *Lt. Jane Army Nurse Writes Home*, as they eagerly awaited their turn. The exclusive story of the fictional Lieutenant Jane was as full of stories about heroic exploits of the Army Nurse Corps as it was about encouraging young ladies to donate to the Red Cross and other charitable organizations until they were old enough to join themselves. The comic appeared in the *Herald* through 1943 and 1944.

Just because women could now enter the armed forces did not mean that typical female roles assigned to them back home were no longer applicable. Along with the constant pressure to attend programs run by demonstration agents teaching proper food preservation, there was the expectation of partaking in local sewing and baking clubs for the benefit of soldiers. And, of course, there was still the Indian Lake Pageant, in which young ladies competed for the crown in front of an all-male panel of judges. There were also subtle—and not so subtle—messages outlining women's responsibilities.

Above: "Lt. Jane Army Nurse Writes to Her Dad" weekly comic strip from the *Denville Herald*. The adventures of Lieutenant Jane were very popular with the young girls in town. *From the* Denville Herald, *November 4, 1943.*

Left: Advertisement from the Denville Herald urging women's patriotism. *From the* Denville Herald, *July 1943.*

"Uncle Sam approves when housewives save while shopping in Denville!" was the Denville Chamber of Commerce slogan for 1942, appearing in full-page advertisements. Let us not forget the Denville Women's Club and its weekly tea party meetings, in which women were encouraged to discuss "topics of female interests."[196] The heavily attended Mrs. Henry Westcott's ninth-grade home economics class in the Denville School was tasked each year around Christmas with baking and sending cookies to soldiers. And when Elanor Johnson was awarded the Miss Indian Lake title in 1944, a little drama ensued in the editorial and mailbag pages of the local paper concerning some male favoritism—specifically in the bathing-suit portion of the ceremony.[197] The dichotomy in women's roles, expectations and perceptions in the war years, especially by the opposite sex, cannot be disputed.

While no cases from Denville were uncovered during this research, one article published in the *Herald* toward the end of the war in 1945 brought up another plight of young women left behind on the home front. "Children's Home Stands Ready to Aid Unwed Girls about to Become Mothers." The inclusion of the article at least shows that this might have been an issue in the small town in Morris County. Across the nation, many women found themselves pregnant when their husbands and loved ones left for the war. Countless children did not meet their fathers, sometimes for years.

Importantly, economic support for servicemen's dependents who were totally dependent on them for support came from the federal government, which provided a monthly allotment check calculated to meet the necessities of life.[198] Subsequently, the uncertainties of life during the conflict exaggerated relations between young men and women. For some women, the uniform seemed to make every boy a man, every man a hero. It is small wonder that the male civilians turned envious of men in uniform and that men in service could not always assess their true relationship with women.[199] Subsequently, World War II increased the number of marriages. In 1941, the marriage rate was 12.6 per 100,000 people, the highest in the United States, with 10 percent of those weddings taking place within three weeks after the attack on Pearl Harbor in December.[200]

The realities for those who found themselves pregnant and unwed were not quite so favorable. This was perhaps the case of a young lady who in December 1943 chose to abandon her baby girl, about ten days old, in a pew at St. Mary's Church. The child was found by a maintenance man when he went to look after the furnace and heard a baby whimpering. There were no clues to the child's parentage. Chief Jenkins reported that labels had been removed from her clothes and a check of recent births in the closest hospital at Dover General failed to reveal any traces.[201] The newspaper ran the story on its front page with the following message: "The mother can easily locate the child—which was placed in a local Catholic family's home by the Morris County Children's Society—if she changes her mind."[202] Perhaps for better, the little girl's mother did not change her mind, and the baby was adopted by the family that chose to take her in. Women lived through the war just as the men did, through sacrifice and sometimes suffering—albeit in their own ways. Yet female contributions to the war effort, whether on faraway battlefields or back home, are not lost to those who followed them.

Part II

OVER THERE

Chapter 6

THE BEGINNING

While local draft boards were organized as far back as 1940—before any American officially fought in the war under the American flag—it was after Pearl Harbor that local boys found themselves being called up in large numbers. As Denville's draft board called for volunteers, the names of sons, fathers, brothers, friends and loved ones began appearing in the *Denville Herald*. Soon the draft board calls turned into announcements of men leaving for training camps. And shortly thereafter, the first casualties began to be reported. The small town sent their boys off with dinners, banquets and social gatherings open to all wanting to attend. A Denville Military Service Committee was formed to see the boys off with all necessities and small gifts. Flags began appearing all over the town center and star signs representing a family member in the armed forces appeared in windows throughout the neighborhoods. Some had as many as four or five stars in their windows. A World War II memorial board was planned for the center of town with the names of all those serving. The boys were ready to go, and Denville's townsfolk were ready to honor their sacrifice and give them the heroes' sendoff that they deserved.

As the draft board was gearing up for a new wave of registration of all Denville men between twenty and forty-five years of age, news of its first son killed in action hit hard. It had been three full weeks since the attack on Pearl Harbor when Mrs. Edward J. Cashman of Bald Hill received the telegram that, deep down in her heart, she was expecting. Technical Sergeant Edward J. Cashman, the brother of the young lady, had been

Ad by the Denville Chamber of
Commerce asking men to join the war.
From the Denville Herald, *March 19, 1942.*

missing since December 7. The telegram was short and to the point.
Sergeant Cashman was killed in action at Hickman Field, adjacent to Pearl
Harbor. He was attached to the Headquarters Squadron of the Eleventh
Bomb Group.[203] He had been connected with the Army Air Corps for
eleven years. The town was in mourning, but it was also inspired. The third
draft call of February 1942 could not have gone smoother. Eight Denville
schoolteachers and several housewives volunteered to give up their time
to assist the local draft board in registering men at the Denville School
auditorium. By the end of the weekend, the draft registry in Denville
gained 325 new men.[204]

    March 1942 witnessed the creation of a Denville Military Committee
chaired by William A. Gardner. The purpose of the committee was to see
that the local selectees were given a sendoff at induction time and were
remembered after they reached camp with gifts and letters, "in order that
they will realize how much their service to the government is appreciated
back in their hometown."[205] When the first group of seven Denville boys
left for their induction on Wednesday, March 18, they were each given
a carton of cigarettes and a fountain pen; by the time the second group
was leaving, the committee added a farewell dinner to the mix. The funds
for the Denville Military Committee came from the local community,
primarily the town's business owners. On April 2, one of the most popular
businesses, Gardner's Soda Shoppe—where the boys now training for war
had just a few months prior carelessly spend their time—had installed a
plaque in their honor for all to see. The circular plaque located in the

storefront window bearing the Denville Honor Roll had excited many comments in the small town. Created personally by Mr. Gardner, it showed the names on a red background surrounded by a circle of blue with white stars. American flags and a Victory poster flanked it. The entire scene rested on red, white and blue satin.[206] It was now nearly five months since the attack in Hawaii; the plaque had fifty-two names on it.

Induction calls by the Denville Draft Board grew each week; seven boys one week, twelve boys another and twenty by June 11, 1942. Announcements for special going-away dinners seemed to multiply on the front pages of the *Denville Herald* each week. As the young men were dined and celebrated at the Wayside Inn, the Fireside Restaurant or the Rockaway River Country Club, receiving a heroes' farewell, the impetus for the celebration was not lost on them. Reports from the early stages of the war against the Japanese were starting to come in. In the Philippines, after the United States surrendered to the Japanese on April 9, 1942, at the Bataan Peninsula, news circulated of a forced sixty-five-mile march of American and Filipino soldiers to prison camps. The exact figures are not known, but historians have agreed that thousands of troops died because of the brutality of their captors, who starved and beat the marchers and bayoneted those too weak to walk. Those who survived were taken by rail after the march to prisoner-of-war camps, where thousands more died from disease, mistreatment and starvation.[207] Private First Class William Van Orden of Denville was reported missing in action according to a telegram from the War Department received by his parents a month after the infamous Bataan Death March.[208] It was not until the end of the war that his parents found out their son had survived the march and was a prisoner of war in one of the infamous Japanese prison camps in the Pacific. For the boys saying their goodbyes with dancing and toasts to glory, the fear of never seeing their loved ones again was heavy on their minds.

Soon, letters started pouring in from the military training facilities scattered throughout the nation. As is often the case with wars, the young were enticed with dreams of heroism and grandeur, even with the possibility of death. They could not get into war fast enough. The following excerpt is from a letter by one of Denville's young men, Corporal Robert Shaffer, Battery A, Twelfth Field Artillery Battalion, Fort Sam Houston, Texas:

> *If all the boys in the armed forces of the United States feel the same way, heaven help our enemies when we get ships enough to take the boys within fighting range.*

As you can see, I'm still here in good old Fort Sam Houston, Texas, just outside of San Antonio. The heat here is terrible and the sweat just rolls off all day. Even though it is hot we don't mind it for we're still waiting to get our chance at the Japs. We here understand that rumors are being circulated around the country that our morale is very low and, on the way, to snapping. As I said in the past [Jim], this is all a pack of lies and from what I can see for myself the morale is higher than it ever was in past armies and wars.

Everyone gets a little tired of waiting, that's true but when we get our teeth into the little [sic] bellies that forced this war on us you can be sure we're going to do our best if it's at the cost of our lives, and we will win.[209]

This perhaps best exemplifies the feeling of the young men who enthusiastically awaited their draft call-ups. It also shows the reason why many did not wait to be drafted and instead chose to enlist. Al Sippel remembered those times vividly, even at the age of ninety-five, his mind sharp. He was so eager to go that he quit school at the age of sixteen, left Denville and joined the navy.

It was different back then. Kids those days could not wait to get old enough to go over. They have a volunteer army now, and most everyone doesn't want to go into the service.

I quit school when I was sixteen. Two weeks before I turned seventeen, I joined and then two weeks later they activated me. Five weeks of boot camp and then they shipped us overseas on Easter Sunday on the Queen Mary. *There were at least six guys from Denville on that ship that I knew of, three army and three navy.*

I was eleven when my father died. We were working in the backyard him and I, and my mother and sister had gone to Newark to go shopping that day. It was a hot day, I was working and helping him on the side with piping (he was a plumber) and he was digging posts, I looked over and he was laying on the ground I took my T-shirt off and shielded his head thinking he had a heat stroke. We did not have a telephone those days, it was the Great Depression, I ran over to Mrs. Hall and she called the doctor. My father had a blood clot; he was dead before he hit the ground. The worst part was my mother and sister coming home because then it was up to me to tell them. I was eleven.

My mother did not have any office skills, so she started baking bread and pies and I would go on a bicycle and deliver it around town and that is how we kept the house.

The reason I am telling you this is because when I enlisted, I needed my mom's permission. My mother had to write a letter that she would allow me to go at that age, and I needed to show a copy of my father's death certificate to prove that he was not around. I tell you; I think she signed….I was the money earner in the family; everything I made I gave to my mother. The government took a portion of my navy pay and added it to her check that she would get, and it came to a pretty decent check. I guess it was like $38 a month that I would make, and my mom would be sent half of that. So that was one of the reasons she let me go.[210]

We tend to forget that the nation was still on the back end of the Great Depression when World War II was starting. As Al pointed out in his interview in 2020, apart from the patriotic factor, for some, there was also the monetary necessity of enlisting.

As his sweetheart Claire Zieger waited for him back home in Cedar Lake, Henry Patterson, having enlisted in the navy in 1943, was shipped off to the Great Lakes for basic training.

It really wasn't training; it was learning how to live with people you do not know. It was marching every day for hours, I learned nothing about the navy but everything about marching.

The day—chief petty officer came in and called out ten names. I was one—I had a watch 12:00 p.m.–4:00 p.m. in the men's room—there will be other guys in there with you but you would not talk to them or you would have problems—that was my first day there. The officer was Chief Simmons and he was a very nice person, he was in charge in our battalion, what a nice guy…he had to hit you like that the first day but he was nice… he stayed with us for the whole seven–eight weeks.

The first day or so that I was there, they told us to get our bathing suits on and it was marching away for hours… and then we walked and walked and then we walked up these steps and got on top and the swimming pool looked so small from up so high up, and they made us jump off. It was to get used to jumping from the ship in case it got hit.

We knew we were going to war; we just didn't know where and when. You did not get a day off in boot camp.

I had a choice, I could be a seaman on the deck (gunner, etc.); I chose to be an engineer. Reason for that is…I was assigned to USS Texas, my first ship. My engineering officer was Commander Bond—his family owned some clothing stores in NYC—when I went down to see him he asked me where I wanted to be and I didn't know the difference between the options so he asked me if I was good with tools, to which I said "yes," and he then told me "good, you will be in the engine room."…That was it.

I don't say that what I had to do was great, but the experience was great. I went once across the Atlantic on the Texas. We took a convoy to Gibraltar and then stayed there a few days and came back. It was an old prewar ship.

When we came back, I was transferred to the Quincy. On the Texas my regular run was in the engine room, and at the battle station I was the loader on the ammunition depot for the sixteen-inch guns. That traveled with me with my new orders.

When I went to the Quincy, it was similar, I had the engine room station, but the battle station was now a loader forty millimeter anti-aircraft guns. When we went on the shakedown cruise, none of us knew where we were going but we wanted to be the best guns of the fleet…when we got the message from the bridge to move the propeller this or that many turns and this many ways, I was very accurate. After this the Captain called the shakedown officer, said he wanted Patterson on the battle station to be on the throttle of the starboard engine, and that is how I got there, and it was fantastic!

I was at sea all the time throughout the war.[211]

His recollections of events that happened nearly seventy years prior to this interview were still very vivid in his mind. "I did what I had to do," he added.

Another Denville boy had quite a different experience. Robert Lake who was part of the Ski Corps at Fort Hale, Colorado, wrote home in June 1943 that they had "laid aside their skis for the summer and had taken up mountain climbing, although there was still some snow on the ground."[212] Robert had spent four months getting into the exclusive branch of the service and had to be recommended by a number of skiing experts in the East.

We live at an altitude of 10,000 feet but have most of our training at 14,000 feet, which included a number of camping trips at temperatures from 40 to 50 degrees below zero. I have had several stretches in the hospital overcoming the effects of the extreme cold and high altitude. One of the most peculiar effects of the high altitude is that it seems to change the voices of the boys completely.[213]

One statement by Russell Darpa, interviewed in Denville in 2020 about his basic training at Fort Monmouth, seems to sum it up best: "My basic

Russ Darpa (*standing*) and his friend, "somewhere" in France. *Courtesy of Russ Darpa.*

training was just about crawling on my hands and knees as they fired bullets over my heard; don't raise your head, they kept on saying."[214] Within a few short weeks, the young men would know better to even think about it. They were ready to go to war.

The numbers of Denville boys in service soon surpassed Gardner's sign capabilities, and the township committee authorized to draw on the Denville Recreation Commission's treasury to erect a board at the empty lot on the corner of Center Street and Broadway, "in order that the names of all men in the armed forces from Denville can be posted for the duration of the war."[215] In fact, the number of boys called up and leaving each week left the Denville Military Committee scrambling to keep up with all the going-away dinners. They still managed, even if the funds were coming in at the last minute. The boys were sent away with sweaters made by the Ladies' Auxiliary of the Denville Fire Department and packages with stationery, pens and cigarettes. Their families were given a service flag. Their names were also added to the new honor roll plaque, whose dedication in Denville Community Church in February 1943 was attended by the families of those on it. By July, the more permanent honor roll display in the center of town had amassed over two hundred names, with sixty-two additional ones added by the end of the year. There was quite an argument in the town. Some believed the honor roll memorial was not up to par—as a wood structure it was simply not permanent enough. Others saw the ease and flexibility the less permanent structure allowed for adding and changing the list of names, its major attribute. While the honor roll was moved and stored in the town hall after the war, it disappeared around the 1970s and has not been seen since. Luckily, the *Denville Herald* reprinted the names of the honor roll in November 1943, providing us with the names of those who fought in the conflict. While some names had been omitted and/or overlooked—also a point of contention at the time—it does provide us today with a nearly complete list of Denville's World War II veterans, at least up to 1943.

The list of those called up reveals some interesting points. Namely, by April 1943, Michael Isel of Indian Lake found himself the father of six enlisted sons, five of whom were already in service and the sixth reporting to the induction station that month. The employee of the Lackawanna Railroad was raising the children himself, as his wife had passed eight years earlier. His six boys ranged in age from twenty-seven down to eighteen and served across three different continents, Africa, Europe and Asia. Mrs. Samuel C. Morris, also of Indian Lake, encountered a similar situation when her four sons enlisted and

Six Isel Boys In Service

ALBERT   WOODROW   EDWARD   JOHN   PAUL   RICHARD

Above: The pictures of the six Isel boys of Denville in service as they appeared in the *Denville Herald*. *From the* Denville Herald, *July 8, 1943.*

Opposite: The only known surviving list of the Denville Honor Roll that was displayed in town. This list was the center of much contention, as it missed many names when it was being printed. Names here are as of July 1943. *From the* Denville Herald, *July 1, 1943.*

DENVILLE
HONOR ROLL
★ SPONSORED BY ★
DENVILLE MERCHANTS

★ ★

Dubois Knapp
Rev. W. G. Sorenson
Donald M. McWilliams
Gordon W. McWilliams
Roger W. McWilliams
Charles E. Headley
Frank A. Headley
Donald F. Cregar
Roy E. Mitchell
William Holzworth
Leonard Davenport
Albert Slohoden
R. Norman Scatchard
Robert E. Scatchard
Kaj Swenson
Alfred E. Greenwood
Edward Rielly
Harold B. Hopler
Orr B. Morris
Paul G. Pascal
Robert M. Samuels
R. Gerken
Eugene S. Hastings
Lloyd Corby
Edmond Halbig
Robert Holt
Harold F. Henn
Edward A. Isel
Albert A. Isel
Woodrow M. Isel
John T. Isel
Edward King
Alfred G. Johnson
Edward H. Lash
Donald A. L. Mayer
Ettore Minervino
Austin Minor
Andre Mayeszet
John A. Mayeszet
J. Luther Miller
Kenneth M. Nichal
William C. Clachner, Jr.
James G. O'Leary
William Frisch
Francis A. Rank
Howard Ryan
John Sullivan
Edward J. Conrad
Angelo Felice
Lawyer S. Young
Herbert Braxton
Charles Heischi, Jr.
Norman A. Mohr

Louis Suk
Arthur Hamilton
Walter Grabinski
Dorothy Feiser
Lois A. Miller
Arthur Wiedman, Jr.
Frederick E. Clark
Dr. E. J. Evans
Samuel H. Edwards, Jr.
Walter H. Donnelly
George Washington
Harry K. Smith
Anthony J. Cozzone
E. W. Ronan
William E. Ayers
Leon Lookingbill
Henry H. Schmidt
Russell S. Weisse
Werner Weibel
Robert N. Lee
Kenneth C. Stanford
Peter Kasten
William L. Apgar
C. J. Mueller
Frederick McGovern
Urban J. Mohr
G. E. Pennington, Jr.
John F. Harrison
Harold R. Mitchell
Charlotte E. Armstrong
Harold E. Peer
George H. Ackerman
W. Arnheiter
David Brocker
Richard Baldo
Donald J. Cregar
Elmer Daly
Charles C. Dodson
Frederick C. Doremus
Richard Fischer
W. J. Fitzsimmons
C. J. Homer
Roy A. Mitchell
George H. Robinson
Edward W. Evans
John E. Egbert
Edward Kine
William Eckler
Charles Prester
Joseph Healey
Robert P. Fennimore
Roy Caykendall
Charles N. Stober

Spencer S. Muller
...aine Cosso
Dominick Frenze
George C. Milk
Robert Evans
Harold Reeves
...an Bauman
Edward J. Smith
...an Reiley
Nicholas Markey
John L. Peer, Jr.
Clarence Hoover
James Edward Jones
Robert Wilson
John Dennis King
Edward G. Dickerson
Henry Heres
Arthur R. Benning
Arthur D. Syska
Harrison Garman
Wallace W. Carey
Henry Frieze
Robert Wayne Orr
Harvey Smith
Herman Riley
James R. Fielding
William C. Holland
Andrew Ketcherick
Philip Saur
...ry Vialard
...Schmidt
James Simpson
...n Amato
...A. Schmidt
Frank L. Jayne
Edward W. Jones
Edmund W. Halbig
Herbert Schulkers
Joseph Vrabel
...in Cohen
...n G. Miller
Edward L. McDonald
Harold F. Van Gieson
...n A. Zieger
...rt Farrand
Woodrow P. Lash
...B. Shaffer
Ray Ratcliff
William Peterson
...ry Frenze
James H. Clark
Harold N. Thomas
Frederick McGovern

William C. Milens
O. Thomas De Lalla
Harold N. Thomas
F. Dennis King
George W. Tustin
John E. Phelan
Howard A. White
Edward H. Conklin
A. W. Strickland
Ralph Poust, Jr.
Leo C. Sammon
George H. Hastings, Jr.
John F. Phillips
Richard Stevens
Raymond Ayres
James L. Steele, Jr.
Edward F. Barrett
Frederick C. Henn, Jr.
Alan E. Henn
Robert G. Zimmerman
Elmer Reily
Harold Hornbeck
Edward Hornbeck
Maud E. Greenwood
Richard Glattly
K. Robert Thompson
Roy Ayres
Arthur V. Hopler
Harry H. Beam
Charles Daniel Peer
Howard Lash
Reginald V. Schmidt
Frank L. Madarasz
James Erickson
Orr Morris
Claude Mooney, Jr.
Albert Cohen
Winfield D. Stromberg
Farnham E. Vanderhoof
James F. Vanderhoof
Herman Samuelson
John E. Whitley
Walter M. McGuire
Herbert Vorden
Robert Wiedman
Robert Cook
William Clark
H. Philip Sauer
Henry H. Jaeger
Harvey K. Smith
Stephen Ketcheric
L. M. Whitten, Jr.
Anthony S. Burke

served through the duration of the war. Thus, the war was a family affair, not just because of the families of soldiers left behind having to sacrifice on the homefront but also because of the sacrifice of the few families that sacrificed all that was dear to them. Many of the names on the honor roll are siblings, or only sons, or even only children—which would normally exclude them from the draft. There is only one explanation for that: they volunteered.

As the United States chose northern Africa in May 1942 as its first official military foray into the war against European fascism, it was from there that first messages began to arrive home. Subsequently, through the establishment of a convoy system of American destroyers protecting Allied shipping, the United States had also entered the Battle of the Atlantic. This resulted in some interesting stories making their way back to Denville. The shipping lanes between the New and the Old Worlds were Britain's lifeline in the war against Hitler. Germany knew that if it could knock Britain out of the war before America's full commitment, it could secure Europe. Within four months of the attack on Pearl Harbor in the Pacific Ocean, the Atlantic was the stage for German U-boats sinking 87 ships. By the summer of 1942, the German wolf packs—or U-boat convoys—had managed to destroy a total of 681 Allied ships in the Atlantic.[216] After being back home in Indian Lake barely a month after sustaining injuries in the Atlantic in June 1942, James Tully gave a harrowing account of the naval war to his townsfolk.

We were loaded with 90,000 barrels of crude oil and were sailing blacked out. Taking no unnecessary chances. On our way west we had sighted a sub, but it dove before we could get within range. But they got us anyway. It was 1:50 on the morning of June 12 when the first torpedo hit. Asleep at the time I was thrown on the floor when it exploded right across from my bunk. It knocked out all the lights, and as I was groping for my life belt [life vest] *a second one hit, only a few seconds after the first. At this I forgot the life belt and got topside as fast as I could. Once on deck, I found the ladder and climbed up to the boat deck messing. Getting up somehow, I saw a boat already in the water, and lowered an emergency chain ladder and climbed down to it. Seventeen of us got into this boat, including the captain. As we pulled away, the third and fourth torpedoes struck, about four minutes after the first two. I thought they were shelling us, but learned it was two more torpedoes. The boat we were in had been smashed on the davits* [crane] *and had been literally blown into the water, but somehow it didn't leak. This was lucky for us because we never could have lowered it in time ourselves.*

Fire started when the last torpedoes hit. This is probably the most terrible part of the whole ordeal—this and the uncertainty of what's going to happen. Flames flared up to at least 75 or 100 feet, and we could see it travel down the whole length of the ship as each storage compartment went up. Then it started spreading out over the water…this was where the men on the other boat were trapped because they were on the leeward side and couldn't get away. We learned later that 14 men had been picked up in life belts after nine and a half hours in the water. These 14 and the 17 in our boat made up the 31 survivors of a crew of 46.

Navy planes flying over the spot 10 hours later reported oil still burning for an area of two miles.[217]

When he believed his burned hands had healed enough, James went back for his renewal papers and returned as part of the American convoy system by 1943. By then, the tide of the Battle of the Atlantic had turned, as the rapid launchings of hundreds of U.S. Liberty ships far outpaced the German ability to sink them.

Meanwhile in Africa, some Denville boys finally found themselves getting into the fight they so desperately longed for. With the famous Battle of Stalingrad raging deep in Soviet Russia between Stalin's and Hitler's forces, the Soviet leader asked for the desperately needed second front to divert the Germans. Instead of springing an invasion on mainland Europe, American general Dwight D. Eisenhower launched Operation Torch, an invasion of Axis-controlled North Africa. In November 1942, some 107,000 Allied troops, the great majority of them American, landed in Casablanca, Oran and Algiers, from which they sped eastward chasing the Afrika Korps led by German general Erwin Rommel, the legendary "Desert Fox."[218] After six months of fighting, the last of the Axis forces surrendered in May 1943, opening the door for U.S. invasions of mainland Europe beginning with Sicily and Italy barely three months later. It was fitting that with Africa being the first official military operation against European fascist powers, it was also one of the first in which Denville boys saw any official action.

March 14, 1943, was Private William E. Flinton's twenty-second birthday. It was also the day that his parents received a message that he had been missing in action. The Denville native was part of the invasion force of North Africa's Oran. It took nearly a year for Mr. and Mrs. Flinton to hear from their son, who was with the field artillery in the African campaign when he went missing. He was not done with the army. After spending the remainder of the war in a German POW camp, the young man rejoined

North Africa, 1943. Denville resident Jerry Schreiber. *Denville Historical Society*.

the armed forces in 1946 and then again in 1956, serving his country in the Korean and Vietnam conflicts. Another young man, Sergeant Robert P. Fennimore, son of George Fennimore of Broadway, "may [have been] the first Denville boy to receive the Order of the Purple Heart in World War II." The decoration, awarded after he was wounded in North Africa, was sent home to his father and displayed in Gardener's servicemen's display window. Interestingly enough, "Sonny"—as Robert was known by those close to him—once again found himself in the hospital later in the war. "When I was in service in Sicily, malaria sent me to the hospital but then I recovered and enjoyed Mediterranean swimming and abundant ice cream,"[219] he wrote to his parents in 1943.

Sergeant Joe Krentisky, who was employed by Peterson's Cake Box in Denville prior to being drafted, found himself a bit of fame when he played a prominent role in a story that appeared in the popular military newspaper *Stars and Stripes*. The story is reprinted below.

It seems Joe is in North Africa and read a piece in the Stars and Stripes suggesting that nowhere in Africa was there Ice Cream and cake to match some that the columnist had tasted in Chicago. And being a baker himself, and a New Jersey man [Denville, to be more precise] *in addition, he took exception, for New Jersey men, bakers in particular, are awfully touchy when somebody tries to tell them that someone has something better than they have, or can do something better than they can. So, he gathered his staff about him and proceeded to turn out some four dozen assorted cookies and a chocolate layer cake that measured a yard across the middle and weighed in the neighborhood of 15 pounds. Another fellow made two and a half gallons of vanilla ice cream. The feast was loaded in a truck and driven to the Stars and Stripes office for sampling and comparison. Sgt. Krenitsky, is a mess sergeant for a signal detachment.*[220]

Not all stories that came back from the front were as lighthearted as Sergeant Krenitsky's. Yet it does show us that the men on the front lines did retain some sense of normalcy, or at least attempted to. As each new day brought news of young men being called up by the draft boards, it also brought stories from the front such as Krenitsky's, Fennimore's and Flinton's. One that stands out in particular is that of a local army medic stationed in North Africa.

The only known photo of the (barely visible) Denville Honor Roll display in World War II (*at far left, behind parked car*). The photograph was taken circa 1944. *Denville Historical Society*.

Sergeant Technician Fourth Grade Harald Mann, brother of Mrs. Walter Van Treck of Denville, spent the holiday season recovering from the front at his sister's house, where he was able to share some stories as a field medic in North Africa. This is a story of his selfish acts in Tunis that earned him not only a Purple Heart but also a Silver Star commendation.

> We landed at Fort Lysutey in French Morocco, without seeing a great deal of action, and a few days later started a march of 1160 miles.
>
> Believe it or not, but the army still gets around a good deal on shoe leather. We carried light packs and covered about 20 miles a day, marching steadily eastward to the Tunisian battle front.
>
> As a medic, I carried no weapons, and I was not required to go into the front lines under fire to bring in the wounded. But in one particular hot engagement I just couldn't stand waiting for things to quiet down, and I went out after injured comrades. There was mortar, artillery, and small arms fire. I succeeded in bringing in 21 men to a relatively safe place in a dry stream bed. One by one.
>
> The Germans evidently were observing the Geneva treaty which established medical aid man as non-combatants.
>
> They could have got me, several times, but none did. Once they captured one of our medics who had a pistol on him contrary to regulations and sent him back with a note to our commanding officer warning that if they caught any more like that they'd be shot as spies. Another time they captured one of our ambulances, with some wounded and a couple of doctors, and let them through.[221]

Although just a handful of these early war stories from Denville veterans survive—the ones presented here potentially being all of them—they do show our men in the thick of the war from the beginning. And as the United States' military campaigns were just starting, there was more news to be expected. Some was bad, and some even worse, but they were all stories of bravery and sacrifice. The men who fought in the European and Pacific theaters, just as those named here in the Battle of the Atlantic and the North Africa campaigns, never saw themselves as heroes. But through learning their stories, we can do just that.

Chapter 7

D-DAY

On June 6, 1944—forever known as D-Day—the Allied forces under the command of General Dwight D. Eisenhower began the long-awaited campaign on the European mainland. More than two million troops stormed Hitler's "Atlantic Wall" on the beaches of Normandy, France. After seven days of fighting, the American and British forces held an eighty-mile strip of France; within a month, they had landed one million troops, 567,000 tons of supplies and 170,000 vehicles.[222] The stories of the Denville men fighting in Europe would not be the same or perhaps not exist at all had the invasion of France not been as successful as it was. Military records show that thousands of men were lost on that day and in the months following the Normandy campaign. As fate would have it, a few Denville boys were there on that Tuesday, June 6, and some are still alive in 2020 to tell the tale.

Samuel Howard Edwards Jr., known as "Lefty" to his friends, a sergeant first class in the U.S. Coast Guard, of Morris Avenue, recorded diary entries about the invasion of Normandy at Utah Beach near St. Mere Eglise. These entries vividly portray the feelings of a sailor under fire. Lefty served as one of the crew on an army personnel attack ship (more commonly known today as a Higgins boat). It is the boat that brought troops and light equipment to the beaches at Normandy, popularized ever since in television and big-budget films about the event.

June 6th, 1944

Today is the day that millions of people have been waiting for. We attacked the beach at St. Mere Eglise. The paratroopers attacked at 01:45 A.M. Then came the barrage from the warships. Next in line were the heavy bombers. They did a magnificent job. We hit the beach at 06:30. So far everything had been exceptionally quiet. We lost a P.C. and a destroyer to shore batteries. Also, ten paratroop planes.

This afternoon we lost a flying fortress that was hit by a rocket. This evening the heavy bombers came back to finish off the Jerries so that the beachhead would be secure. We lost five bombers so far, guess the worse is yet to come.

June 7th, 1944

The battle continued today with renewed velocity. More troops were landed with their supplies. The casualties are coming off the beachhead in a steady stream. We are paying heavily for this beach. We lost another destroyer this morning, and two P.C.'s and two LCT's.

June 8th, 1944

This morning we lost two destroyers. One received three direct hits. The other was hit amid ships but was towed in by salvage tugs. These tugs are doing an extraordinary job salvaging all types of craft from the smallest LST's and warships. The Jerries sowed mines last night and they are taking quite a toll. An LST hit a mine and the salvage tugs helped her back to the beach. Casualties were taken to a hospital ship waiting offshore. A British magnetic mine sweeper struck a mine and sank in 20 seconds…a British coaster hit a mine and went down in about 2 minutes.…

Tonight, Jerry came over again bombing the beach, and then he hunted for the supply ships. The ships scared them off with terrible anti-aircraft fire.

June 9th, 1944

This morning a new convoy arrived. The beachhead is progressing rapidly. Prisoners are coming out by the boatloads. The engineers are building a pier out of sunken ships. When this is completed the big artillery will be brought in and the enemy will be driven back with great rapidity. The cruisers have been shelling the beach and inland continuously, not giving the enemy a chance to get their big guns back into action.…

The troops are now advancing rapidly with the aid of big guns of cruisers and battleships. The ships are coming in a continuous stream now. Unloading troops and supplies, and going back for more.

June 14th, 1944
More and more troops and supplies coming in. Never saw so many. The Germans will have a poor chance when these men get started. All types of boats are bringing them in…ships, ships everywhere as far as the eye can see. What a sight.

June 15th, 1944
Just when we thought it was over. The Jerries bombed the beach under the light of many flares. One plane made a dive at us and missed by about 50 feet.…It gives one a queer feeling while watching a plane diving on you. When one hit the beach the concussion would throw us off our feet.[223]

Lefty's diary goes on to June 23, 1944, until the young man finally proclaims, "The beach is clear of debris now and the ships are unloading without any interference." While many mistakenly assume that the Normandy invasion was just a single day on June 6, it was in fact a multiweek operation, as evidenced by the notes taken by one of Denville's own.

Al Sipple admitted in an interview in 2020 that he still felt that none of the supposed pictures taken and seen on documentaries on TV from the first day of the invasion of Omaha Beach are real. "They look too calm…all the people in the pictures would have either been tripping over dead bodies or be dead themselves." Al was also part of a crew of an LST (landing ship tank), a ship created to support amphibious operations by carrying heavy equipment and landing troops directly to shores without docks.

Our boat was three hundred feet long and fifty feet wide and carried twenty Sherman tanks and then there would be an elevator right inside the bow doors and they could raise things up to the main deck and they would put half-tracks and Jeeps up there, small artillery, ambulances… some LSTs had two LCVPs and some had six, we had six. LCVP was a small boat [also known as a Higgins boat; infantry can be seen leaving these boats to get to the beach in photographs]. *They carried about thirty-five fully equipped infantry or a Jeep; there was a three-man crew, a coxswain and motor machinist and ramp operator. I was the ramp operator.*

On D-Day we went in there on our [Higgins boat] *to bring the U.S. Army First Combat Engineers to the beach. We all got shot at with machine gun bullets right away. The boat next to us, they lowered the ramp in front of a German machine gun nest and it killed everyone in the boat, thirty-eight men, every single person; they never even got a chance to get out of the boat, I will never forget seeing that. They actually found one guy alive under there, but he was shot four times; but they took him to a hospital ship, and he survived.*

We got in on the beach about 8:00 a.m. You cannot imagine what it was like…the bloodiest five hours of any battle that I had ever been in. It was hard to describe.…It makes you want to cry. The only people that you could talk to about this that would ever understand would be the ones that were there. And there are not many of us left. On D-Day they dropped us off about eight miles out and it was about a three-hour ride to get to the beach, myself as the ramp operator and the two other navy crew, plus the soldiers we were bringing to Omaha. It had to be eight miles out because that way you would be out of the 88s German guns' reach. That boat had a flat bow, so it would not cut through the water, so it took a while. We were also fully loaded with army GIs. The three hours seemed forever.

On that day we made only one trip in. On our way in there, there was ships around us sinking because they had hit mines. We ran into about five guys swimming in the water. Their boat had hit a mine and blew up, and our coxswain slowed down and we tried taking them on board; we only brought two on because we couldn't bring the other three as it would sink the Higgins boat. We had to leave them there…you just must make yourself believe that another boat did come and pick them up; but you never know. When we got to the beach, it was really hard for us to find a place to land because everything was so wrecked there. We finally found a place. I opened the ramp and our men got out. Bullets hit and a few of them got shot right away. Some of them were not killed, just wounded, and got themselves propped up on some floating dead bodies so they did not drown. When we got unloaded the coxswain said to me, "crank up that ramp, we are getting to hell out of here." I said, 'What about those two guys out there?' He says, "My orders are not to pick up any wounded." He wouldn't let us crack down the ramp but did give the motor machinist and I a few moments. So, we jumped in the water and he got one by the collar and I got the other, and we dragged them back and pulled them in. We took them to a hospital ship on our way back to the LST. I do not know if they lived or died. We did not really know any of the army men we were transporting.

Altogether, it was my five hours of Omaha Beach invasion.

That evening back on the bigger LST, we were laying out and waiting for orders and this German bomber came out and nobody shot at him. He came over our bow and we fired and set him on fire and the guy inside the plane jumped out and he was on fire from his head to his toes. We must have hit the gas tanks. It was all on top of us when the plane blew up...all this stuff fell on us from the sky.

The next day, my gun was on the port side, I oversaw that gun when on the LST. And when it was light, I noticed that the wheel from the blown-up plane was laying there...it missed me by about ten feet. We scrapped the metal and rubber from the wheel. I took a piece of the wheel to have in memory, but I lost it over the years.

We made nineteen trips across the English Channel in total transporting men and equipment after D-Day.[224]

Al used to never share his story of D-Day until he was at a doctor's office when already in his nineties and picked up a magazine in which he read that people were forgetting about the significance and human sacrifice of the Normandy invasion. From that day, he swore to himself that he would share his story if ever asked.

Storekeeper Third Class Denis King, a twenty-two-year-old from Indian Lake, and engine room machinist Henry Patterson, twenty years old at the time and of Cedar Lake, both experienced the war from the deck of a brand-new American cruiser, the *Quincy*. King told his story while home on a fifteen-day furlough in 1944. Patterson related his story from his apartment in Denville seventy-six years later.

Before Normandy, the *Quincy* and its crew were in Belfast, Ireland, where General Eisenhower inspected the ship. He seemed greatly impressed with the efficiency and comfort of the most up-to-date model of an American fighting ship, recalled King. "The boys all knew they were getting ready for an invasion, but of course we couldn't tell our families," added the young sailor.[225] One could not miss the fact that something was happening. "There were ships everywhere with more and more coming each day," recalled Mr. Patterson many years later.[226] "Boys" was the right word for the crew, too. They were nearly all between seventeen and twenty-five years old, with a sprinkling of old-time petty officers to keep them in line. On D-Day, the *Quincy* was anchored off Carentan, about six miles out, at 2:00 a.m. The crew could not see the beach being bombed. Their ship began firing about ten minutes after the enemy stared shelling the fleet from shore. When the ship responded, it did so in style, commented King.

Right: Hank Patterson. The inscription to Claire reads, "Loads of love to the sweetest girl a fellow could know, Henry." *Courtesy of Hank Patterson.*

Opposite: Russ Darpa still has his German-English Dictionary, which he carried with his gear throughout the war. *Courtesy of Russ Darpa.*

Her eight-inch guns, aided by perfect coordination between fire control parties ashore and plane spotters in the air, showed the Germans what naval marksmanship could do. We got the first target with the second salvo [simultaneous firing of artillery], *the second target with the third salvo, and the third on the very first salvo. Later on, we hit a motor convoy eight or ten miles inland—14 to 16 miles from the ship and wrecked a mass of German trucks.*[227]

The next morning, Henry Patterson looked out into the water around the ship; it was full of debris and dead bodies. "They asked us if anyone would volunteer to help go in the water to collect some of the bodies; I volunteered." He finished his recollection of D-Day by adding, "Us engineers on the *Quincy* were like brothers. After the war we got together for many years; we went to reunions and kept in touch. I am the only one left."[228]

Russ Darpa, interviewed while staying at the same senior home in Denville as Hank Patterson, choked up when recalling his experience on Omaha Beach. Russ was the Message Center Chief of the Sixth Army and was part

of the sixth wave to land on Omaha on June 6. Darpa and Patterson often meet for coffee and laugh at the idea that Hank was shooting over Russ's head on that day as the latter was storming the beach—and they did not know of each other's existence.

> *I was apprehensive. They directed us off the ship and put us into the loading barges* [Higgins boats] *and we had all this equipment on our bodies. When we got close to the shore, they put the landing gates down, but we were not in low water. We came across so many bodies and debris floating around. A friend of mine disappeared right next to me; he was too heavy with his gear on and couldn't find any footing. We had to hold on to the debris and the bodies to get to a point where we could stand. And of course, there was still shots being fired at us.*
>
> *After things quieted down a bit that night, we saw people being put into body bags. We called them the "grave company." And then we got in line. They marched us through a town and directed us to an open field with hedgerows, and that is where we slept that first night after invading France.*[229]

Watching the two men talk about their experiences and feeding off of each other was quite breathtaking. Both men viewed the events of that day as something that just was, not a heroic act, but more of a hope—hope that the war would eventually end and they could go home.

Speaking of home, the celebration of D-Day was planned in Denville well before the event occurred. A front-page article in the *Denville Herald* of May 18, 1944, outlined the "D" Day Prayer Service that was to be held on Broadway the morning of the invasion. In case of rain, the festivities were to be held inside the Denville Theatre. While the specific date was not known, it was agreed by the Denville Town Council that the town celebration was to take place the morning the news of the invasion of Europe was announced. Thus, on June 6, 1944, at 9:30 a.m., church bells sounded in Denville announcing that the prayer service was to take place at 10:00 a.m. in the center of town on Broadway between the traffic light and Center Street.[230] As Girl Scouts and Boys Scouts wore their uniforms and carried American flags, a truck with a platform was procured and heads of the community's churches—regardless of the denomination—led the townsfolk in a prayer. Afraid to say it out loud, the people of Denville, just like Henry and Russ over on the other side of the world, one on a naval ship and the other on the beach, knew that this was the moment they would all look to as the turning point of the war.

Chapter 8

NEWS OF OUR MEN IN UNIFORM

Europe

Your fathers shed their blood for you; Their fathers did the same.
And yet this world has still not learned that war has a bloody name.
This world is O! so greedy; and men just crave for fame.
No matter how they get it; they'd kill just for a name.
Now Hitler wants to conquer and Mussolini, too.
But we and our allies know greed is just taboo.
When all these wars are over and once again there's peace
Let's hope and let us pray for a world of love, for keeps[231]
—Olive Morris, ninth grade, Denville Junior High School, October 1942

Before the battle for North Africa was won, the Allied commanders commenced operations for the invasion of Europe. Taking British prime minister Winston Churchill's recommendation to attack through Italy instead of France—as was suggested by the American commanders—the Allies began their Italian campaign with the capture of Sicily in 1943. The mainland invasion of Italy followed that same year. With Hitler choosing to stop the Allies in Italy instead of Germany, the effort to completely liberate the nation did not come to fruition until mere months before the complete Nazi surrender in May 1945. By June 1944, the Allies had also finally—and successfully—opened another European front in France with the famous D-Day invasion of Normandy. By September 1944, American and British forces had liberated the nation, made headway into Belgium and raced toward Germany. Denville men were there each and every step of the way. Here are their stories.

Located in a folder at the Denville Museum is a photo of an unidentified Denville man fighting in Italy. The folder contains other photos of men from the town who have not yet been identified. *Denville Historical Society.*

Mr. and Mrs. Headley of Union Hill received an interesting letter from their son Technician Corporal Everett Headley with allied troops in Sicily. He gave a graphic account of the difficulties in waging mechanized warfare in the rugged and mountainous terrain of the island and of the pitiful condition of the inhabitants, who were practically destitute of food and clothing.

> *The old people especially look so starved and hopeless that the Americans eat only a part of their rations in order to share them with the Sicilians. One feature of the Allied occupation that amazes the population here is the fact that the troops lie town in the streets to sleep, having no tents, whereas the Axis soldiers drove the citizens out of their homes so that they themselves might be comfortably housed.*[232]

Another Denville son, Sergeant John Dominick, moved to Denville—which he called his "real home"—in the 1930s to work at St. Francis Health Resort. He enlisted on February 6, 1942, and was decorated with the Silver Star for gallantry in action in Sicily. The citation reads as follows:

John P. Dominick, Sergeant Company "G," 40th Engineer Combat Regiment, for gallantry in action. On July 10, 1943, northwest of Scoglitti, Sicily, Sergeant Dominick was a member of a reconnaissance party ordered to locate a suitable beach exit road. While crossing a stretch of flat terrain, the party encountered a group of six enemy soldiers. Although exposed to enemy fire, Sergeant Dominick crept to cover of a low stone wall and proceeded to a point of less than twenty-five feet from the group.

He then rose to a position from which he could deliver submachine gun fire, shot one of the enemy, and forced the others to surrender. By his courage and initiative in a moment of great danger, Sergeant Dominick enabled his party to complete its mission.[233]

The order was signed by Lieutenant Colonel O.B. Beasley, commander of the regiment. In a letter to his friend Franz Zahn, also of Denville, the twenty-eight-year-old Dominick expressed his wish to be back home and back at work. His wish was granted in late 1944, but not until Sergeant Dominick and his friends had found themselves bogged down in the next stage of the war, the invasion of Italy.

In their fight against the Nazis, the U.S. forces unleashed an air campaign that the world had never seen. Beginning with flying missions in Italy, then France and, eventually, Germany, the bombings were so intense that, according to modern research, they sent shockwaves all the way to the edge of space and briefly weakened the outermost layer of Earth's atmosphere, known as the ionosphere.[234] In all, Allied bombing raids left their devastating mark on Germany, killing more than 400,000 civilians and laying waste to entire cities, from Berlin to Hamburg to Dresden.[235] What made these missions so dangerous was the fact that, unlike the British RAF, which conducted its missions at night to lessen British aviator casualties, the Americans made their flights during the day for best visibility and target accuracy. In turn, this made being part of the U.S. Army Air Corps— eventually Army Air Force—one of the most dangerous jobs in the war. During the entirety

Sergeant John Dominick of Denville. The picture shows the young man after he received his Silver Star for a reconnaissance mission in Sicily. *From the* Denville Herald, *November 18, 1943.*

of the conflict, the United States lost an average of 170 planes per day.[236] These grim statistics, together with the history of the pilots who flew them, provide us with a glimpse of the dreary and downright scary job of being a pilot and/or a plane's crewman during World War II. Beginning with Italy and extending all the way to bombing missions in Germany, the Denville boys were there operating in the skies above Europe.

Lieutenant Richard Glattly was twenty-two when he was awarded the Air Medal for meritorious achievement while participating in an aerial flight in the Italian campaign. The young man from Denville was a navigator in a B-17 Flying Fortress. In a period of five weeks in 1944, the young man flew twenty combat missions, which, considering the statistics of bombers being short down daily, was indeed extraordinary.[237] Another local recipient of the Air Medal in the Italian campaign was George W. Tustin, a flight surgical technician of a troop carrier wing. His citation describes "meritorious achievement while participating in aerial flight; for professional skill and devotion to duty in evacuating sick and wounded from the combat zone." The young man was a member of one of two medical air evacuation squadrons, components of the wing, who had evacuated more than 170,000 patients during the invasions of Sicily and Italy up to December 1944.[238] Unfortunately, Lieutenant Glattly's life ended just short of his twenty-third birthday when his plane was shot down by enemy fire shortly after he was awarded his Air Medal. His name appears next to those of the other ten young men from Denville who made the supreme sacrifice in World War II.

As Master Sergeant Chris J. Mueller Jr. of Rock Ridge in Denville woke up on Monday morning in France, he could still remember assisting his father in operating a machinist's shop as a teenager. When news of Pearl Harbor hit the airwaves, Chris was one of the first boys to enlist from Denville. Because of his knack for fixing things and his experience, he was trained as an air mechanic. After his training in Texas, the young man was assigned to a B-29 group operating from England. He was eventually moved to France in support of ground forces driving into Germany. As his young wife, Vivian, awaited his V-Mail letters, young Chris was rising through the ranks of the U.S. Army Air Force. By 1944, Sergeant Mueller became the flight chief who supervised maintenance work for each flight of Marauders that went out from the Ninth Air Force Bomber Base, first in England and then in France.[239] On him rested the responsibility for having the medium bombers ready to fly every time a mission was called. One of Chris's classmates at the Denville School, Master Sergeant Santhoff, found himself in a similar position, as an aircraft engineering chief on the P-51 Mustang fighters for the Eighth Air Force Fighter Station in Britain. The air war was a combined effort of those who serviced and prepared the planes and those who flew them. The small Morris County town could claim to have taken part in both.

Near Sergeant Santhoff's base in England was another classmate, Second Lieutenant Robert M. Samuels of Cedar Lake, stationed at the Eighth Air Force Bomber Station. He was twenty-three years old in 1944 and already a copilot on the crew of a B-17 Flying Fortress. His "courage, coolness and skill and his outstanding performance of duty during a number of Eighth Air Force attacks on German targets," had earned him his third Oak Leaf Cluster, added to the Air Medal he already had. But "Bobby," as he was known to his friends, was not quite done with his exploits behind the controls of his B-17 bomber, which he christened *Pursuit of Happiness*. Within months of his award, Lieutenant Samuels earned another commendation and a promotion from second to first lieutenant. His parents back in Denville were notified of his heroism of piloting his bomber and leading his section of planes onto the target despite the loss of one engine in an Eighth Air Force attack on oil refineries at Merseburg, Germany, in November 1944. Just before turning onto the target area, a burst of flak caught the Flying Fortress, knocking one of its engines out of commission. Determined to avoid breaking up the formation they were leading, Lieutenant Samuels and his copilot held the crippled bomber steady until the bomb run was completed, enabling the entire formation to drop its explosives in a tight pattern on the target.[240]

Bobby's group was cited as "crew of the week" by their group operations officer. Bobby's action climaxed a long record of similar examples of devotion to duty on the part of the crew of *Pursuit of Happiness*. "During more than 30 missions," the citation read in part, "this crew has exhibited outstanding ability and dependability. Flying in the lead of a flight, they have repeatedly taken their aircraft over the target under adverse conditions."[241] Lieutenant Samuels's unit, the 480th Bomb Group, was a member of the 8th Air Force's famed 3rd Bombardment Division, the division cited by the president for its epic shuttle-bombing attack on the Messerschmitt factories at Regensburg, Germany.

The real liberation of Europe began with the American forces overcoming German resistance in Normandy, France, from which they poured into the mainland. On July 25, 1944, General Omar Bradley unleashed a massive bombardment against the enemy at St. Lo, France, providing a gap in the German line of defense through which General George Patton and his Third Army could advance.[242] Within a month, the American forces liberated the French capital from over four years of German occupation, followed by the complete liberation of the nation in September. In fact, by the end of the September 1944, the United States and its allies had freed France, Belgium and Luxemburg. By the following month, the American forces had taken their first German town, Aachen, sparking Hitler's last stand, more commonly known as the Battle of the Bulge. The battle to recapture the Belgian port of Antwerp and push the Allies back raged for a month. After driving their tanks sixty miles into the Allied territories—creating a bulge in the lines—the Germans were pushed back. Not much seemed to change in the Germans' situation from before October. Yet, the battle proved to be very decisive. The Germans had lost 120,000 troops, 600 tanks and assault guns and 1,600 planes; soldiers and weapons they could not replace.[243] From that point forward, the German forces could do nothing but retreat ahead of the advancing Allied armies entering the German fatherland.

News of the Denville men seemed to come from the front at a faster pace from mid-1944. They ranged from heroic deeds to wounds suffered in combat, as well as individuals making the ultimate sacrifice. Mr. and Mrs. Theodore Jensen of East Shore Drive received word from the War Department in Washington, D.C., in November 1944 that their son Private Royden Jensen, Infantry, was seriously injured earlier that month with General Patton's Third Army. With presumably no hope of their son making a full recovery, the couple was relieved when they received a second letter, this time from their son barely a week later. Writing from his hospital bed, he informed them that they would soon be receiving his Purple Heart in the mail. Unfortunately for many parents, that second letter never arrived.

Two best friends from childhood, Austin Minor and Alfred Newman, were well known around Indian Lake as happy-go-lucky kids and, eventually, tactful young adults. When the United States entered the war in December 1941, the two young men decided to enlist, Austin in the U.S. Army and Alfred in the U.S. Marine Corps. Minor's family saw it as a bit of a surprise, as the young man was an honors student all through high school and even won a full scholarship to Syracuse University. Yet for Austin Minor, that did not seem to matter. He chose to forgo college in favor of working at a defense plant and shortly thereafter enlist in the army. It needs to be mentioned that Austin was in a sense an all-American boy, an athlete and a scholar who in his high school career won many honors, including the Roosevelt Memorial Medal, American Legion Award, excellence in scholarship award, French Institute Medal, English Medal and the Habuermeyer Memorial for Scholarship.[244] After his basic training, he was noticed by his commanding officer and recommended for OCS (Officer's Training), but he once again declined, this time saying that he did not want to abandon his buddies in his unit with whom he had made close relationships.

And so, the young Denville man arrived in England in August 1942. In November, he took part in the invasion of Africa and in the Tunisian campaign. Minor then made the landings in Sicily and Italy before he was again commended and sent back to England for further training. He once again declined officer training and a promotion and found himself participating in the invasion of Normandy on D-Day. When his sweetheart, Claire Maloney of Myers Avenue, received a letter from Austin dated September 15, 1944, neither of them knew that the all-American athlete, scholar and soldier would be mortally wounded just two days later. He was hit by a bullet from a German sniper rifle while in Belgium with the First Division of the First U.S. Army.[245] Sadly, nearly a year before, he had lost his "dearest friend" on Bougainville Island, New Guinea, in the Pacific theater. Sergeant Austin Minor and Private Alfred Newman were finally reunited after not seeing each other since enlisting in 1942—albeit this time in a different place.

While in retrospect we can look at the timeline and see the war in Europe entering its final stages in 1945, it did not seem to be the case to those still fighting in it. The same could be said of their relatives back home. Mr. and Mrs. Norman Cook of Richwood Place were notified by a telegram from the War Department of the death of their only son, Private First Class Robert James Cook, on January 1, 1945, in Luxembourg. He was fighting with General Patton's Third Army.[246] The death of Private Carroll Roleson, who was killed in France on January 10, 1945, shook many in the small town. His lovely young wife and his one-year-old, Carrol Jr., were always seen around town. Mrs. Roleson volunteered her time to many war-effort initiatives, such as the Red Cross. Even though the young couple had just moved to Denville in December 1941, after the United States was already at war, they quickly became town favorites to those who knew them. Private Roleson was twenty-six years old at the time of his death and was with the Sixty-Eighth Armored Infantry.[247] The townsfolk held a memorial service for Carrol at Denville Community Church three months after his death. The collection gathered at the Mass was donated to his young wife and son.[248]

The European theater of the war was not done taking the lives of Denville boys. Mr. and Mrs. Kenneth R Mackenzie of Cedar Lake received the dreaded telegram in the first week of April 1945. Sergeant Robert E. Mackenzie died of wounds in a hospital in Germany on September 23, 1944. The young man had escaped death just a year before while serving in the Thirty-Fifth Infantry Division under General Patton, even sending his Purple Heart to his parents with a note proclaiming it must not have been his time.[249] He was not so lucky when he was reported missing in action while on a special mission near Agencourt, France. He was later found mortally wounded and was transferred to a hospital in Germany. He died the next day.

Concurrent with the stories of ultimate sacrifice, the folks back home began receiving news of their young sons' exploits with the U.S. armed forces rapidly moving toward Germany. Private Claudio Mooney, a wireman and telephone operator who repeatedly laid, serviced and repaired field telephones for Patton's Third Army, was awarded the Bronze Star. He had done his job as a wireman under artillery and small-arms fire "during which he displayed outstanding leadership and courage and was always ready to volunteer to repair vital communication lines." The twenty-year-old Denville man told his parents that he would often be sent out "under the cover of darkness, mortar fire, machine gun and rifle fire," adding, "I just tried to stay calm."[250]

Robert Fennimore once again wrote to his parents, two months prior to the German surrender in June 1945. He talked about meeting other Denville men and his prognosis for the end of the war.

> I am writing this letter in behalf of Bill Clark and myself....We are in France with the Seventh Army. It is a beautiful country we are seeing but in no way compares with our beautiful town of Denville. The [Denville] Herald reaches us here regularly and we both enjoy it very much....I had even met Ralph Ford over here and it was a grand reunion. I have not seen him since we enlisted. The war looks really bright for us in the present. The Russians are knocking at the gates of Berlin and I hope they will be in by the time this letter reaches you. The Germans are fighting very hard and our victory will come the hard way. The Germans are good fighters and even craftier ones, so we fellows are not being optimistic.[251]

While Fennimore was getting his well-earned rest, John Harm was also in France, where he was about to be credited with taking down a Nazi tank. Private First Class Harm was awarded the Combat Infantryman's Badge at the Battle of Bitche, where he and eighteen others of his platoon knocked out a German tank. Crossing the Woher River under fire from the tank, the young man and his brothers in arms managed to get close enough to the tank to retire it.[252]

When the Battle of the Bulge began, the surprise factor and the speed with which the Germans were able to smash through the American lines left everyone on the front lines rattled and scrambling. Master Sergeant Charles A. Hirschi of the Twenty-Eighth Infantry Division stationed in Luxemburg during that winter of 1944 instead acted calmly and accordingly, which earned the Denville man a Bronze Star citation.

> *Sergant Hirschi's efficiency and outstanding devotion to duty as Chief Clerk of the Adjutant General's Department is highly commendable. His knowledge of the operation of administrative procedures of an infantry division under combat conditions has proven to be of inestimable value. Due to Sergeant Hirschi's organizing ability, the written records of the Division were successfully evacuated from Wiltz, Luxemburg during the German winter offensive of 1944. He and his depleted staff labored to the point of exhaustion to protect valuable files and irreplaceable equipment during subsequent movements of Division Headquarters.*[253]

The citation went on to add that young Hirschi's pleasing personality had won him the friendship and admiration of his associates.

There are two other interesting stories of local men who received some attention back home. One local boy, part of Company C, 302nd Infantry Regiment making its way through Germany, left quite a mark on his brothers in arms as well as on his superiors. Sergeant Frank J. MacKain took it upon himself to rally his friends in turning what might have been their last action of the war into one that earned them a bit of fame. When his company occupied defensive positions on the Rhine River, his mortar observation post was attacked by a strong enemy combat patrol. Quickly perceiving the situation, Frank led a bold charge against the Germans and, to his own surprise, forced the attackers to retreat in complete panic and disorder. In the end, the chase led to the Denville man capturing eight Germans, who could not do much but stare at the daring young man whose charge had left even his own men behind and trying to catch up.[254] Another case that made news back home was that of Private First Class Arthur Strathman, who temporarily resigned his post on the Denville Police Department to join the army. Little did he know that he would take on a very similar job overseas. Assigned to the Military Police Platoon, 76th Infantry Division, Art was placed in command of the traffic squad, which was responsible for directing the traffic of hundreds of military transports of personnel and equipment, sometimes under fire. It was due to his calmness and ability to dispatch his assigned duties under heavy enemy fire that the Denville police officer earned the Bronze Star.[255] Officer Strathman returned to Denville after the war and resumed his position on the police force, becoming the town's chief of police in the 1950s.

As the war in Europe was nearing its end and more boys began to come home—at least temporarily, as they were being readied for the final push against Japan in the Pacific—many stories from the front arrived with them. Listening to Lynn Reiley of Indian Lake talk about his experiences in Europe is interesting, not because he saw or did anything different or startling, but because he translated the campaigns he participated in—Normandy, northern France, central Europe and Germany—from printed generality to unpleasant actuality. In an interview given shortly after being discharged in 1945, the young man stated:

> *I served on a C-47 Hospital plane of the 91st Medical Air Evacuation Transport flying casualties from trenches to hospitals.*
>
> *I spent considerable time in France. Although I thought the Parisians were all right, I was more favorably impressed by the French peasants in the outlying districts who would give you the shirts off their backs. I made a lot of friends among these people.*
>
> *Overall, the French, while fairly well clothed, were desperate for food, soap, cigarettes. They threw ridiculous amounts of good currency at passing American soldiers, in hopes of receiving some of the desired commodities in exchange. The women would walk right up to you and beg for soap.*
>
> *I visited a German concentration camp at Weimar a few days after it had been taken. I saw heaps of bodies—some of them freshly killed, many of them women and children. The people in the country around, acted as though they never had known the camp existed. I guess they were afraid.*[256]

Arriving back home, Lynn spent most of his time reading newspaper and magazine stories about the war. He was pleased with the general accuracy of most of them. "It was a tough grind. But I am glad to be home," he added.

First Lieutenant Ralph Vogt wrote a letter to his parents back in Denville while he was stationed in Germany in June 1945. In it, he described what he saw with his own eyes in German prison camps:

> *All the ones we've come across were really horrible, although none had more than a few G.I.'s in them. Believe me, those pictures you have been seeing are far from exaggerations. In fact, they can't begin to show how*

bad these places are. You've got to see 800 half dead skeletons crammed into a small shed, see them with sores and filth all over them and thighs like my wrists, see the gas chambers, the big oven crematories, the chains where they tied men stripped in the snow and threw water on them, see the little solitary cells where men went crazy; see skinny naked bodies stacked like corn-wood and dumped into graves dug by a bulldozer, see the rock quarries where men carried huge loads till they dropped and then were pushed over a 300 foot cliff just for the hell of it, see the worn-away stone wall where men were shot for dropping out of line after standing at attention for three or four hours, and most of all you've got to smell the filth and disease when men haven't the strength to move from their lousy little spot on the floor. And why were hundreds of thousands put in places like this? They didn't commit any terrible crime; they weren't captured fighting. They just didn't think right; they didn't like our little friend Adolph.[257]

Some of those returning from Europe had indeed much different stories to tell. The atrocities they witnessed no doubt stayed with them forever. For several Denville men, the nightmare was all too real, as they spent some if not most of their time overseas as German prisoners of war.

While at least eleven Denville families received letters and telegrams that ensured their pain and loss would be everlasting, other families were left in limbo, as they were notified of their loved ones' status as prisoners of war.

Dear Miss McCarter,

Your brother Pfc. Harold McCarter, who has been reported to you as missing in action is in all probability a prisoner of war in Germany. The details of the incident in which he and others were captured must, of military necessity, remain secret till the war with Germany is completed....

Pfc. McCarter was a soldier in my company, and I had opportunity to witness the fine work he was doing during operation in France and Belgium. I can't say more than—I am proud he was in my company and I am praying for a quick finish of this war so I may meet him in Germany and bring the happy word back to you.

We have faith in your brother's safety—you must also have faith.[258]

This letter, from her brother's commanding officer, arrived on October 21, 1944, and was followed a few days later by the official confirmation from the U.S. government of her brother's status as a POW.

Mrs. E.C. Flinton of Denville had perhaps the best of surprises on June 6, 1945, when her son rang the doorbell that evening and walked into her living room unannounced. William Flinton was a prisoner of war in Stalag 2-B in northern Germany until liberated by the Americans. The last his mother had heard from him was in 1942, nearly three years prior to him walking through her door. "The conditions in the prisoner camp weren't too good, but weren't too bad, as the life-saving Red Cross packages came through without being looted. I was mostly put to work on a farm under guard. Just before Germany collapsed, one day we were told to march. We marched 400 miles to keep from being freed by the Russians."[259]

Another Denville ex-Nazi prisoner was promoted to staff sergeant and was awarded the Bronze Star. George Blaine was initially reported missing in action during the Battle of the Bulge in Belgium. His young wife and mother of three young children, Helen, was beside herself when the rumor of his death proved to be false, when she received a letter from a German prison camp a month later in January 1945. After serving months in Stalag 4-B in Muelberg, Germany, George and his fellow prisoners were "locked in a boxcar and left where American bombers were at work." His German captors fled from the U.S. forces closing in on them.[260]

Lieutenant Louis Amster, a member of the Italy-based Sixteenth Air Force, spoke at the Rockaway-Denville Rotary Club in early December 1944. He related his experiences of being a German prisoner of war in occupied Romania.

I had to bail out at 18,000 feet when two motors of my plane died. It was an awful shock when the parachute opened, snapping me to what seemed like a dead stop in mid-air, and the rest of the trip down was uneventful. Crowds of Romanian peasants saw me coming and were practically on the spot when I landed, whereupon they followed out their orders and apprehended me and then delivered me to German military authorities.

The food provided in the prison camp wasn't bad but could have been a lot better. We were told that was the best to be had, but during the week between the time we were liberated and then picked up to be returned to American forces, we discovered that there was plenty of food outside.

Some American made articles the prisoners had with them sold at high prices, such was the case with $3 for a pack of cigarettes. Others like the expensive aviator's watch that my brother had given to me, went for a mere $6, as Romanians had plenty of Swiss watches and the demand wasn't high.

> *A couple of Chicago boys tried to get away by beating up a civilian who they thought had the keys to an automobile. He didn't have the keys, however, so they returned to camp. A little later the civil authorities came to the camp with a warrant; it seemed the men responsible were to be tried for assaulting a civilian. But as their identity wasn't known, we all managed to save them from further trouble by swapping dog tags and having a couple of other fellows hide in an attic during roll calls. From then on, until we were all freed, the officer in charge of the camp thought he had two less than were actually in our enclosure.*[261]

Amster's experience, as well as those of others who came back from the European theater, was as much unique as it was part of the greater story of American GIs overseas. Through the stories of these men, we get a glimpse into the major battles and happenings in the fight to defeat fascist governments and liberate the continent of Europe. Yet, even in the darkest of times, there was still room for local boys to have some light moments and even find love on the old continent.

STAFF SERGEANT SAMUEL J. Amato came back to Cisco Road in Denville in October 1944. Instead of being elated about his return, he was saddened by the fact that his British wife was still a month away from her trip stateside. When the former Miss Campbell finally arrived, the young couple settled in Sam's parents' home and started a family. Their story is yet another in a series of unique GI experiences. Along with instances of young soldiers meeting their future wives in the female auxiliary branches of the U.S. military, there were circumstances of falling in love with local women. In the case of Denville men, it was both.

First Lieutenant Russel Weisse of Denville married First Lieutenant Katherine Weight, Army Nurse Corps, of Guthrie, Kentucky, on December 8, 1944. Interestingly, their marriage was the first known wedding of an American soldier in Belgium in World War II. For another Denville man, it may not have been wedding bells, but it was perhaps just as exciting. "It was the most unusual of my war experiences," stated Ed Lash of Morris Avenue when a picture of him being kissed by a Hollywood movie star, Myrna Loy, graced the pages of the *Denville Herald* in the February 15, 1945 issue. The young man happened to be recovering in an army hospital in Australia when the silver-screen vixen visited as part of celebrations conducted by USO, an organization that provided recreation services for the U.S. armed forces.

On the other side of the spectrum were romances between local women and American soldiers stationed in their countries throughout the war. Such was the case with Staff Sergeant Amato and his wife, Edna Campbell, of Yorkshire, England. Restrictions were so tight that when they were married, they received just enough time on leave for the wedding and no time at all for a wedding trip. Their story in the *Herald* pointed out how the groom had contributed heavily to the revenues of the British railway system and sundry taxi operators, traveling between the big air depot where Russel was stationed and Ely, England, where his bride was quartered.

> *The trip from camp to Ely and back usually involved a bike or a truck ride of ten miles from my camp to the nearest railroad station, then a train trip of 30 miles, and then of course the return. Nights I caught a ride on a truck as I had no bike to get back on. The other guys and I on the late train would charter a taxi, paying a dollar a piece for the ride. The train got in at 12:30 a.m. and passes were valid only until 1:00 a.m., so we rarely made camp on time but the M.P.s were very understanding, and the deadline was never enforced.*
>
> *I met my wife at a Saturday night dance in Ely. One of the English civilian units comparable to our Denville air raid wardens or police reserves, sponsored the affair. Edna caught my notice because she was much prettier than the average English girl. I think most English girls suffer by comparison with American young women because their climate doesn't give them as much sunshine and because war shortages have put the people on such a lean diet. I really don't know how they get along on those rations of two ounces of butter a week, one egg every two weeks, meat at two meals a week, even tea scarce.[262]*

Miss Campbell was one of an estimated seventy thousand British war brides who arrived in the United States from 1945 to 1950, tens of thousands of whom, like Edna, were transported here by the U.S. Army.[263]

Speaking to Winn Hill in 2020, almost eighty years after she met and married a GI in England, she gives the feeling that it happened yesterday. After the war, the couple chose to settle in Denville and start a family.

> *Bill was in the 816th Engineers, stationed at an air base in England. While he was there, my future husband and some friends got together and formed a band, the "Yankee Serenaders." They would play in the villages around the base. The Army would send out trucks around and bring us*

girls back to the base, where we would spend the evening dancing. I was one of those girls.

Where I lived, we had about fifteen airports all around us....Flying Fortress, Spitfires, Marauders, we had them all. One night they had a dance at the field, and it was close to Thanksgiving, so they invited us girls to the dance. I happen to know one of the officers and he invited me to go. Well during the intermission, I noticed this guy standing up that was in the band, and I liked his looks. He looked at me and then he excused himself and came down to speak to me and asked me if I would like to go to the movies sometime. We were only together for ten days when he asked me to marry him. He met my parents and we were all set to have a wedding. He was able to get some leave from the station, and because he was friends with some army cooks form Pennsylvania, they were able to supply us with food for the wedding. I made my dress out of parachute silk that I was able to get through my job, which was a silk manufacturer for the army.

Up to three weeks before D-Day, Bill played in the band and stayed at the base, but then he was called up for D-Day and he shipped off. I did not see him again for a year.[264]

Winn was able to secure a ticket to the States but was told she had to get to Liverpool and ship off the next day, which led to some rushed goodbyes. Her in-laws, whom she never met, picked her up from the port, and she lived with them for almost a year before she again saw the husband she barely knew. They remained happily married until his death many years later.

Chapter 9

NEWS OF OUR MEN IN UNIFORM

Pacific

Through stormy weather and mountainous wave; a small P.T. sped so brave.
Through torrent incline and corral reefed waters; the P.T. speeds, but never falters.
Each man at his action post; waiting to do his utmost.
On sight of the stealthy foe; the torpedoman jumps to the torpedo.
With his expert once over, he received the command; then releases torpedo with his skilled hands.
With a hiss and a swish, it's a perfect shot; sending to the bottom another filthy lot.
The nimble gunner mans his machine guns; to keep the enemy planes on the run
These miniature battleships shall never fail; always blazing for us the victory trail.
—John Bosk, eighth grade, Denville Junior High School, November 12, 1942.

Although the Allies had agreed that the defeat of the Nazis was the prime objective in the war, the United States wasted no time in starting its own war against Japan. In the first six months after Pearl Harbor, the Japanese conquered an empire that dwarfed Hitler's Third Reich. On the Asian mainland, Japanese troops overran Hong Kong, French Indochina, Malaya, Burma, Thailand and much of China; they also swept south and east across the Pacific, conquering the Dutch East Indies, Guam, Wake Island, the Solomon Islands and countless other outposts, including two islands in the Aleutian chain, which were part of Alaska.[265] The war against Japan can best be defined as naval forces battling over the vast Pacific Ocean in the early stages, then the long American campaign

Photo of Walter Mutz from his days in the Pacific theater. *Courtesy of Walter Mutz.*

of island hopping to get within striking distance of Japan's home islands by seizing strategically important islands. By adopting the latter strategy, the U.S. Navy commanders were able to bypass strongly held Japanese islands and isolate them with naval and air power—further allowing the American forces to move rapidly toward Japan.[266] Author of *D-Days in the Pacific*, Donald L. Miller, stated that, as D-Day is military code for the beginning of any offensive operation, in the Pacific theater during World War II, there were more than one hundred D-Days.[267] As with the European theater, Denville men found themselves in the thick of things.

Sergeant Raymond Caporaso's sister, of Hussa Road, received the following letter from her brother's commanding officer in the Pacific. Ray had been at Pearl Harbor when the Japanese hit the island, and by the date of the letter, June 1943, he had been involved in action on Guadalcanal for six months.

Dear Hilda,

Having heard so much about you from Sgt. Caporaso, I feel as I know you. As the Sergeant's platoon leader and in gratitude for the splendid service he has given to his country, I feel that his family should know about a few of his achievements. "Cap" as the company affectionately knows him by has proven himself to be our squad leader. Time and time again his courage and resourcefulness have enabled my platoon to accomplish its mission.

I know that you will be interested in a few of his exploits. One thing about battle, it enables a leader to gauge the caliber of his men and to determine their worth by their deeds. What do YOU think about your brother? Our platoon had the difficult job of attacking a ridge which was strongly held by the enemy, so as to create a diversion and allow the main part of the battalion to encircle the Japs and take them from the rear. Forward we went but were pinned down by machine guns. Two of my squads returned the fire while I held "Cap's" squad back. Then I gave him the order to assault the ridge while the other two squads supported him by fire. We shook hands and the sergeant moved out, at the head of his men, he swept on up the hill, grenadeing a machine-gun position out on the way up. It was a magnificent charge and it carried the day for us.

Another day I was instructed by the Company Commander to pick two crack squads with the job of cleaning an area for five hundred yards in front of our positions. We had already killed fifty Japs there, and there were an undetermined number left. It was our [sic] job to find out and eliminate them if possible. I picked Sgt. Caporaso's squad and another of the second platoon. I explained our mission and stated that if anyone didn't relish the task they could stay back. Not a man stirred. Is it any wonder that we officers are proud of the American soldier? As a result of that little sortie, we killed six Japanese soldiers; took eight prisoners, captured an 87mm, anti-tank gun, a platoon battle standard (which "Cap" now has as he took it) and stores of supplies. It was a very successful raid.

I could go on for pages…but these two incidents will give you an idea of your brother's service.…Your brother typifies the fighter that will save our country.…There can be no doubt as to the ultimate victory.…Please don't think me forward writing to you like this, but I feel as if it is only a small thing I can do for a man who has done so much for me.

[signed] *Lt. Robert W. Leonard*[268]

While many of those who fought were not always keen on sharing the stories of their war exploits, loved ones were sometimes pleasantly surprised to hear the tales from unconventional sources, or even newspapers.

Instead of writing to his family, William R. Ackerman, Sergeant Second Class, U.S. Navy, wrote a letter to the *Denville Herald* from his new station, "Island X somewhere in the Pacific," to thank folks back home for thinking of him. "As a lot of my Denville friends sent Christmas cards that I could not return the greeting to, I want to thank one and all for thinking of me…; I suppose that people of Denville are having trouble keeping their cars and houses from freezing while we here are having trouble finding a way to keep our barracks cool."[269] The paper published other secondhand accounts of friends writing to the paper on behalf of Denville men. Apparently, the *Herald* made its way to the front and was often shared by the soldiers, whether they were from the New Jersey town or not. Through editorials such as those in the "Mail Bag" section, we learned that Sergeant Arthur Wiedman of Franklin Road was "digging a foxhole in the jungle when a coconut fell from a tree, striking him and fracturing three ribs."[270]

Sergeant Robert Shaffer of Denville left his job as a printer helper at the *Denville Herald* in January 1942; he did not see his hometown until fifty-six months later. The young man came back in 1945 with four Pacific campaign stars. Robert served in, among others, New Zealand, Guadalcanal, New Guinea and Leyte. Attached to the Air Inspector General's office, Shaffer shared some of what he witnessed on his travels. "Enemy bombing raids numbered from one a month to six times a night at various points. I once saw a Jap suicide pilot take down five B-24 Liberators. Another time, I had to take to the foxhole when raiders mistook a new coral road through a camp area for an airstrip and laid a string down the middle and into the camp post office, blowing up all Christmas mail and packages."[271]

Shaffer's long time in the Pacific's Island-Hopping Campaign was almost as impressive as the career of Lieutenant Raymond Coykendall of Diamond Spring Road, who accumulated thirteen thousand combat hours with the famous Thirty-Second Red Arrow Division. The unit's history is filled with stand-up fights in which they had little or no support—wearing the Red Arrow patch signifying that the division had pierced every line it had encountered.[272] With 654 days of combat in New Guinea and the Philippines, Shaffer's unit had the most time in combat of any American division in the war. The young man remembered often finding himself "taking over higher responsibilities when most of my superior officers, from colonel down to captain, were killed."[273]

As was the case in Europe, the Denville boys operated in the skies above the Pacific. Within months of Pearl Harbor, Mrs. Steward Chambers received notification of her son Captain Chambers's decorations of the Silver Star for gallantry and the Distinguished Service Cross with Oak Leaf Cluster for having shot down three Japanese planes in his first official mission out of his base in Australia.[274] Working on the ground maintaining B-24 Liberator bombers was U.S. Army Air Force corporal Ludwig Halbig of Pocono Road. "Day and night, we are on hand at the jungle air strip with other members of my team waiting to meet the returning bombers. The damage of the day's raid is repaired immediately, and the planes are made ready for an emergency takeoff."[275] Similarly, Staff Sergeant Leonard Davenport announced through a letter to his parents his honors of having successfully flown sixty-eight missions (in six months) as a gunner on a B-24 Liberator while stationed in China with the Fourteenth Air Force.[276]

Davenport came back to Denville in August 1944 after completing an eight-month tour of duty in the China-Burma-India theater. In the end, the twenty-three-year-old flew eighty missions, some over Rangoon, Canton, Hong Kong and Hangkaw, and was credited with shooting down one enemy plane and four probables as a gunner on his B-24.

My last mission was the most unlucky. The [plane] had been somewhat shot up and we had difficulty in finding our home field. So, after two hours of hunting for it, our crew bailed out. We all reached the ground in fairly good shape, except the pilot, who was hurt when he landed in a tree. We then walked 150 miles back to base. It took us a week, during which we lived mostly on rice, boiled, with sometimes a little chicken soup to keep it from being too dry and flavorless. When we couldn't get chicken soup, we used potato water. I don't care if I never eat rice again.

Another time, I found my turret and gun mechanism out of commission, so I opened the door to get at my guns. I had to stand up and lean out to reach them and was working the bugs out when a Jap plane came from nowhere and sent a slug almost vertically up through the gunner's seat. If I had been occupying the seat in the usual position, I'd have gotten that bullet right in the seat of my pants. Fortunately, the Jap didn't follow up his temporary advantage, and the ship got home safely.

Life on the field was pretty monotonous. We played baseball and cards— the latter being pretty costly sometimes—read books from the library and hang around the non-commissioned officers' club. There were some Red Cross girls at the base, but the commissioned officers had the advantage with them. Wine and women were what we missed the most, and those with girlfriends would get bothered if they didn't get letters so regularly as they thought they should.[277]

After returning home, the young man looked forward to home-cooked meals. Until his death in 1987, the U.S. Air Force sergeant never forgot the time his broken gun saved his life.

The island-hopping campaign of the Pacific sped up the necessity for, and the creation of, the U.S. Naval Construction Battalions, more commonly known as Seabees. The need for building staging bases, air strips and even bridges as the armed forces sped their way toward Japan by capturing strategic islands, made Seabees one of the most crucial military groups. The work was difficult due not only to time constraints, but as Carpenter Second Class John F. Phillips of Denville recalled, "the temperatures [in the Pacific] would get as high as 135 degrees as we worked."[278] At least three Denville men were part of Seabees units scattered throughout the Pacific. William Edilch of Union Hill proclaimed: "The Seabees have about the ideal middle ground of the armed services. The Navy men have to spend so much time on ship and the Army so much time ashore that neither branch gets around so much and enjoys so much variety as the Seabees."[279] Yet it was by no means a fun experience to be part of the construction battalion, nor was it free of danger. Edilch himself admitted to having spent two nights in his dug-up foxhole, which he later found out was dead center inside a mine field. He survived, but the same could not be said for another Denville Seabee, John F. Phillips, who died in the South Pacific from a heart attack after having just survived a harrowing mission.

Unidentified Denville soldier back home from the front. Denville Library at the time of war is seen in the background. *Denville Historical Society.*

As mentioned earlier, the Pacific theater was full of D-Days; none were more infamous than the invasions of Iwo Jima and Okinawa. After retaking much of the Philippines and liberating American POWs, the Allies turned to Iwo Jima, an island that writer William Manchester later described as "an ugly, smelly glob of cold lava squatting in a surly ocean."[280] Made famous because of the photograph of U.S. Marines lifting the American flag on one of its peaks, the island's importance cannot be overstated. Controlling it would allow Allied heavy bombers to reach mainland Japan in a continuous loop. It was also perhaps the most heavily defended spot on the planet, with 20,700 Japanese troops entrenched in tunnels and caves. Only 200 survived the Allied onslaught when it was all said and done.[281] In the end, over 6,000 Americans lost their lives taking the island. As with prior invasions, Denville was well represented in the effort.

Private Richard "Dick" McNally (USMC) of Summit Road, Denville, was eighteen years old when he found himself living in foxholes for twenty-five days during the invasion of Iwo Jima. Yet his inability to change his clothes and the quickly depleting K rations were nothing compared to the pain and loss he felt losing two of his good friends in the last days of fighting on the island.[282] They never even saw who fired the shots that killed them, both presumably dying by sniper fire within a span of two days. It appears that Dick McNally did not share all of his stories from Iwo Jima. His older brother Private Frank McNally Jr. provided the rest in a letter dated April 1945.

> *I received a letter from* [my brother] *last week in which he told of a very interesting experience he underwent while on Iwo....It seems that Dick was walking along when he came upon three Japs, apparently dead. Two were dead and the third was just feigning death. Dick noticed his neat appearance and immediately shot him through the shoulder. The Jap jumped up and came at him, only to receive the rest of the clip through the head.*
>
> *Dick stated that this was one of the last three Japs he knows he killed personally. I don't imagine he mentioned this to anyone else because Dick is like that. I do believe that perhaps some of his friends would like to know just one of the experiences that our brothers go through.*
>
> *Dick also said that we don't want to laugh at the Jap soldier because he proved on Iwo that he is a force to be reckoned with. When a Jap sniper drew a* [target] *on a Marine, that boy was a dead Marine.*
>
> *Perhaps in some respects this might be a tip-off on how long the Pacific war is going to take.*[283]

While the younger McNally might have been too modest to share his near-death experience, his brother most certainly was not. Dick McNally lived to tell the tale after the war, but there is no public record of him ever doing so.

Another Denville boy, Private First Class Henry Jaeger (USMC), spent his twenty-eight days of the bloody campaign on a special assignment: going into the battle area to make sketches of men in action as the company's artist. Nineteen of Henry's drawings had been sent back to Washington, from which they likely appeared in various publications.[284] Unfortunately, no surviving art by Private First Class Jaeger had been located at the time of this research. On the other hand, evidence points to Henry surviving the invasion and making his way back home to marry his sweetheart in 1948. Not everyone was so lucky. In the end, at least one local man lost his life in the bloody attack at Iwo Jima. Private First Class Edward Hornbeck (USMC) of Lake Arrowhead was killed in action on February 28, 1945; he was nineteen years old.

The last major battle of the Pacific theater—and the first on the mainland Japanese islands—was the Battle of Okinawa in April 1945. It was one of the bloodiest battles of the conflict, as the Japanese unleashed more than 1,900 kamikaze attacks on the Allies, sinking thirty ships, damaging more than three hundred others and killing almost 5,000 seamen.[285] That was only the beginning. As the Americans came ashore, the invasion claimed nearly eight thousand American lives. The Japanese paid an even bigger price, with 110,000 lives lost, a total that included two generals who chose ritual suicide over the shame of surrender.[286] Based on the lives lost and the determination of the Japanese to defend their home islands, it was predicted that 1,000,000 American lives would be lost if a full-fledged invasion of Japan was to take place. That was the main catalyst for President Harry Truman's decision to drop the atomic bombs on Japan. It was at Okinawa where Corporal James J. Moran (USMC) found himself volunteering to undertake what proved to be a dangerous, daylight reconnaissance of enemy-held territory. Alone in the territory that his regiment was to operate in, Moran and his fellow men were able to avoid enemy patrols and gather information that was deemed by the Sixth Marine Division as "accurate, comprehensive, and of great value to the assault and supply units that subsequently operated in the region."[287] The Denville youth's actions earned him the Bronze Star.

Perhaps more interesting is the fact that Moran was with the first patrol to enter the capital city of Naha in Okinawa. For more than an hour on the afternoon of May 13, they explored the northernmost ward of the city, separated from the main part of the town by the broad mudflats of the Asato Estuary. Three men from the patrol attempted to cross the mudflats with covering fire by Moran and others of the patrol but were foiled by what seemed to be quicksand. "We felt awfully lonely down there. We had entered the town from the west, skirting the base of the bluff, crossing a long row of tombs, and coming upon a deserted street….We didn't see any Japanese as we crossed two more blocks to reach the river. This part of town was in shambles, with nearly every building beaten in by the artillery."[288] The honor of being the first Americans to enter a Japanese city since the outbreak of the war rested lightly on the marine, who modestly called it "just another patrol."

Thus, just as Denville boys were there at the beginning of the war with the Battle of the Atlantic, they were also there near the end, with the taking of Okinawa. With Japan still possessing a massive army and its resolve stronger than ever—as evidenced on Okinawa—President Truman saw only one way to avoid an all-out invasion. Ultimately, the president decided to take advantage of the work undertaken by scientists working on the Manhattan Project and employ the still top-secret atomic weapons. On August 6, a B-19 named *Enola Gay* released an atomic bomb, code-named "Little Boy," over Hiroshima. Forty-three seconds later, the city ceased to exist. When the Japanese leadership failed to surrender, a second bomb, this one code-named "Fat Man," was dropped on Nagasaki. This time, there was no hesitation. The Japanese emperor admitted defeat. The war was over.

Part III
BACK HOME

Chapter 10

VE AND VJ DAYS BRING
NEW ANXIETIES

The summer of 1945 brought to Denville the news of both VE Day (Victory in Europe Day) and VJ Day (Victory in Japan Day). Along with rejoicing and celebrations, the news brought with it fears and concerns of a postwar world. For the small New Jersey town, getting back to normal included the creation of a new organization that would ease the reintroduction of soldiers to civilian life, the creation of a local Veterans of Foreign Wars chapter and the construction of a permanent war memorial. As local businesses began restocking and reopening without OPA guidelines and factories eased back into civilian production, the people of Denville were ready for the war to be over. James Whiton perhaps summarized it best in his editorial of November 1, 1945.

In reading and re-reading [of the letters that our soldiers had sent to me], *I became more and more conscious of the responsibility that is mine, as an individual beneficiary of their self-sacrifice, to do my full part to make certain that these boys and girls shall return to a home town that will measure up in every respect to the home coming they have dreamed about in foxholes, on missions over Germany and Japan, in enemy infested waters, and in long lonely hours spent on hospital beds all over the world. Through it all, the one thing that has served more than anything else to make any situation endurable has been the thought of coming home. Yes, my friends, they had a job to do—a job to do for you and for me, and how well they did that job you know as well as I. And the only reward they ask is the privilege of coming home to take up their lives where they left off in the kind of community, they, by their united effort, have made possible.*[289]

The townsfolk left behind fought their own version of the war, as did their loved ones overseas. In a sense, it was time for everyone to come home.

Before any news arrived regarding the end of the war in Europe, Denville announced—nearly a month before VE Day—plans to hold a thanksgiving service on Broadway following the announcement of victory in Europe, one similar to the prayer service held after the announcement of the invasion in Normandy. On Saturday evening, April 28, 1945, news came over the radio that Germany had surrendered. The report was quickly squashed, with a *Denville Herald* editorial going so far as using the event to highlight the superiority of newspapers over the speed of unchecked radio news. When the real news finally arrived via an announcement by President Truman on Tuesday morning, May 8, 1945, open-air services were held under the Denville Theatre marquee. The Cedar Lake public address system was borrowed to carry the words of Reverend Charles Mend, Father Sullivan of St. Francis Health Resort and Benjamin Greenwood, chairman of arrangements.[290] As businesses in town closed and Broadway was filled with people attending a huge outdoor celebration, Greenwood read a prayer written by Mrs. M.F. Hunt of the Undenominational Church. The day of festivities ended with special services at night at both St. Mary's Church and Denville Community Church. While not completely over, the war's end was no longer an impossible dream.

When news of the dropping of the atomic bombs was made public, the people of Denville had mixed feelings. Yet, there was a consensus that dropping the bombs was necessary to bringing their loved ones home. Still, the debate that still rages to this day began almost immediately after the decision to use the bomb was made. "Would You?" asked a headline in the *Denville Herald*. "The big headlines and the editorials and sermons are all devoted to the destruction and slaughter being wrecked on Japan and the human beings there…but what about the boys whose lives will be sacrificed if we go on with the task of subduing Japan by what is now the old-fashioned method, with Superfortresses and B-24s in the air and mortars and machine guns and beachheads on land?" The article ended with, "Would you, if you were President Truman…want to face one of your countrymen and say, 'I sacrificed your boy in order to spare a [Japanese]?'"[291] Needless to say, even at the time, while controversial, the

FOR GOD AND COUNTRY

DEDICATED IN HONOR OF
THOSE WHO SERVED IN ALL
THE WARS OF THE UNITED STATES
AND
IN GRATEFUL MEMORY OF THOSE
WHO MADE THE SUPREME SACRIFICE

WORLD WAR NO. 1
HARCOURT, JACK   PEER, JAMES A.

WORLD WAR NO. II
BERDONE, CHARLES V.   MACKENZIE, ROBERT E.
BRODZIAK, PHILIP   MINOR, AUSTIN J.
COOK, ROBERT   NEWMAN, ALFRED E.
CLATTLY, RICHARD J.   PHILIPS, JOHN E.
HENNING, CHARLES E.   ROLESON, C. W.
HOGAN, ROBERT J.

KOREAN WAR
CLARK, WALTER JR.

IN HUMBLE HOMAGE
FROM
THE PEOPLE OF THE TOWNSHIP OF DENVILLE

Honors plaque detailing
those who died in
the world wars, as it
appeared in 1955.
Denville Historical Society.

people of Denville were behind their president. Their reward was an end to the bloodiest conflict the world had ever seen.

As reported by the local paper on Thursday, August 17, 1945, the announcement of Japan's surrender two nights prior at 7:00 p.m. "started a modified, local version of the Times Square celebration at the center of Denville."[292] The article reported that whether it was because of the smaller number of people or because county folks just naturally have better sense than city dwellers, there wasn't much crazy behavior—for which the police were thankful. "By 8 o'clock there were a couple hundred people gathered at the Point [corner of Broadway, Main Street and Diamond Spring Road], where boys raced about towing tin cans on bicycles and one or two autos with mufflers disconnected added blasts to the racket."[293] With the crowd perfectly orderly, the police officers, Chief Jenkins and Patrolman John Kelly, were able to lead an impromptu parade. It also helped with keeping lawfulness that the governor of New Jersey ordered all taverns closed from Tuesday night to Wednesday at noon. Still, news did not reach the police in town until close to 10:00 p.m., thus some patrons were able to celebrate properly, with pre-purchased alcohol. The next morning saw a thanksgiving service like the ones from the Normandy invasion and VE Days. That same night, Denville townsfolk attended a standing-room-only service at Community Church that was attended by residents of all faiths and denominations. The services were followed by "a torchlight parade and general hilarity, which lasted well into the morning hours."

As the Denville Local Defense Council voted to close its control center and discontinue its light and telephone service on Tuesday, May 29, 1945, one could already see the town's rebirth. A month before, the Denville Grill, which had taken a hiatus amid the OPA regulations and rationing, reopened its doors and "resume[d] serving the same agility foods of the past, together with the usual courteous service of its personnel."[294] It was not long before other businesses followed. As reported in the papers, "another indication of Denville's back-to-business-as-usual program for the post-war era [was] the announcement today of the re-opening Cornell's Tea Room." The oldest business on Broadway—it first opened its doors in 1929—was one of the town's favorite restaurants and was soon known throughout all of Morris and neighboring counties. "Like many of the business concerns, the coming of the war presented so many new problems to Cornell's that the management decided to close temporarily rather than render a service that was not in keeping with their established policy of serving the finest food."[295] "Happy Days Are Here Again!" screamed a headline in the classifieds page of the local paper. Another read, "OPA Release…Now Ration Free! Fine Leather Shoes without Coupons!"[296] And, of course, there were the ads. "Now on Display: The Car That's Really New; The 1946 Oldsmobile at Lynch Chevrolet in Denville/Rockaway!"[297] Between advertisements indicating normalcy, one could also see the replacement of columns about Victory gardens and news of men and women overseas with articles on veterans and offering advice, as well as advertisements for the services of those returning from the front.

As U.S. federal offices were set up for veterans, offering advice and employment aid throughout the state, Denville created its own Military Service Association (MSA) to make the process a bit more personal for the returning men and women. The purpose of the association was "to render service to men and women in the armed forces and merchant marine and to assist them in establishing themselves in civilian life after they are released from service, to aid and advise their families, and to work for a permanent war memorial."[298] Apart from helping steer the veterans in the right direction when seeking jobs, home loans and/or higher education, the MSA also sponsored various benefit dinners for returning vets and donated money to their families, if they were in need. Another big aspect of the association was raising funds for a more permanent war memorial, which was decided to be a new township library. The project, which called for raising $40,000, was intended to be a living memorial to those of Denville who had served in the armed forces. The fundraiser was kicked off with a parade around the central part of town with music, sermons by St. Mary's pastor and fire engine sirens. The library was finally built in 1952 on Diamond Spring Road with the Denville Memorial Fund for Soldiers. Its meeting room was also used by the American Legion and the Veterans of Foreign Wars until they erected their own buildings.[299] Edward Lash of the U.S. Army was the first World War II member to join the new VFW post, on September 20, 1945.

With the vets returning home, there were many calls for giving them job priority. The Denville Public Works Department held positions and appointments for returning veterans; other township departments soon followed suit, as did local businesses. "Men—Men; Get you post war job

Denville Memorial Library as it appeared in the 1960s. The library has since been moved to a new building. *Denville Historical Society*.

now!" called the ad for the Montville Chemical Works published in the *Denville Herald*. There was indeed fear of postwar unemployment that needed to be quelled. George Benson made the issue more exasperating in his "Looking Ahead" column in the local paper. "Specters of unemployment shaped in the smoke of war are scary…the street corner estimate is that 20 million people will lose their jobs."[300] The issue did hit close to home. Denville's VFW held an interest meeting in October 1945 centered on the situation at Picatinny Arsenal. "The drastic curtailment from 18,000 to 500 employees, affecting as it does the local communities, the returning job seeking veterans, and the security of the nation, was reviewed in open discussion."[301] The Denville VFW Post felt that the government of the United States should have set a good example in reemploying returning veterans who had worked for it before the war; something that it failed to do. It should also be noted that prior to the U.S. entrance into the war in 1941, the plant employed four thousand workers.

There were indeed many questions left unanswered, and not many answers were readily available. Once again, the *Deville Herald*'s editorial pages provided a glimpse of local people's concerns.

> For the past nearly four years, most of us have been taking orders one way or another about whether we would work or not, and for what employer.… There was strong control and direction with War Manpower and War Labor Board regulations on one side and Selective Service on the other and rationing all around everything else.
>
> Now, we will be free of those compulsions. What are we going to do? Rationing, for instance. No more gas coupons needed—are we going to go over unnecessary driving and unnecessary speeds? The V-J News didn't improve the quality of the tires on our cars one bit, nor did it suspend the laws of physics. And about those blue points? Are the foods they used to protect going to be grabbed up so fast that we have an inflation in our Denville groceries?
>
> And War Bonds? Are they going to be inflation fuel, or will they be held for a real emergency?
>
> And our attitude toward Government? Have we got so used to working for it that we still expect it to provide us all with jobs and overtime pay checks? An article in the Saturday Evening Post notes that a great many service men hope to land in the security of civil service jobs. Obviously, there can't be enough of those to go around unless we start nationalizing, socializing, a lot of business and industry.[302]

The concerns of the local people were not without merit. More than anything, there was a real fear of uncertainty and the unknown. After all, the nation and its people had been still very much getting over the Great Depression when the war started, and hence there was a legitimate fear of the nation plunging right back into it.

The war-bloated economy was losing steam. By October 1945, some 300,000 war plant workers had lost their jobs. The unemployment was even more felt than before, as paychecks had doubled in size—up from an average of twenty-six dollars a week in 1939 to fifty-two dollars a week in 1944.[303] A lot of the jobs lost belonged to women, who now had to relinquish their newfound freedoms to the returning men. In the end, more than two and a half million New Jersey lives had been altered by the conflict—half a million by military service and two million by war work in factories or other war-connected tasks within the state.[304]

What ultimately saved the nation and its people from plunging back into the Great Depression were the massive shortages of peacetime goods from the times of rationing and government regulation. People, who now had money saved from working in war industries for the past four years, created a market that production companies were willing to fill with goods. Everything from tires, cars, furniture, refrigerators, toasters and houses were needed and purchased at what seemed lightning speed. Coupled with the postwar baby boom, a new demand rose for child products such as diapers, baby food, clothes and schoolbooks—even station wagons. With these new demands came new expectations of a better life, a careless life. In a sense, the war had saved the people and allowed them to have better lives. A New Jersey historian probably said it best: "The twentieth century was nearly at the mid-point. The second half would make the first half seem almost as distant as ancient Greece and Rome."[305]

EPILOGUE

If I learned anything from the World War II research presented here, it is that there is always hope. Even in the darkest of times—and, perhaps, specifically in the darkest of times—people find a way to come together. And when we are together, we can do anything. The story of the small town of Denville, New Jersey, and its people in the greatest conflict the world had ever seen has taught us just that. James Whiton, the main editor of the *Denville Herald*, wrote the following in the last issue of 1945—the year that saw our nation, as well as the nations of the world, defeat an unimaginable evil.

> *Now that Christmas is past, we come to another day of greeting. It is just as easy to shout, "Happy New Year" as it was to carol "Merry Christmas," but what does it mean? Is it just a conventional form of words like "How are you?" muttered to a passerby whom you scarcely recognize? Or, realizing that happiness does not come as easily as sunshine after rain, that happiness has to be earned by our own efforts, can we sincerely and confidently invoke happiness for our people?*
>
> *There is so much in prospect that will make for unhappiness that we often doubt or wonder. In world affairs we have a ruined Europe and Japan, and large areas elsewhere seriously damaged. Millions are dead, other millions are wounded in mind or body, and yet more millions are starving and homeless. Open suspicion and smoldering hatreds block the path to peace. Racial and religious friction and economic competition are setting group against group. Can this bring happiness?*

Located in a World War II folder at the Denville Museum is a photo of soldiers (one presumably from Denville). The inscription on the back reads, "To Mom." *Denville Historical Society*.

Our recent wartime experience has proven (if the history of our people had not previously done so) that cooperation brings larger rewards than conflict does; that we are all citizens of one world and that this world is meant to be run on the principles set forth in the Sermon on the Mount and summarized in the Golden Rule. We may deny it, or evade it, or give it only hypocritical lip service, but we cannot escape it.

The problems of the world are primarily moral rather than political, economic, or social.

Only by admitting this fact and applying it to our own personal conduct in home, community, and state, can we work with the law of the universe. We honestly believe that each year sees greater recognition of this fact, and finds more people trying to be good neighbors in spite of those who do not try.

As the tensions bred by the war subside, the goal of human brotherhood will be recognized as worth greater effort and will be more nearly achieved. And in that belief and hope and trust, we sincerely wish you a HAPPY NEW YEAR!"[306]

NOTES

Introduction

1. Geoffrey C. Ward, *The War: An Intimate History* (New York: Alfred A. Knopf), 72.
2. "It's Pulling Together That Counts," *Denville Herald*, March 28, 1944, 5.
3. "Everybody's Business Is Our Business," *Denville Herald*, April 20, 1944, 5.

Chapter 1

4. "How Franklin Roosevelt Lied America into War," accessed April 10, 2020, http://www.ihr.org/jhr/v14/v14n6p19_Chamberlin.html.
5. John Cunningham, *New Jersey: A Mirror on America* (New Jersey: Afton Publishing, 1978), 309.
6. Ibid.
7. "History—World War II," accessed April 10, 2020, https://www.newjerseyalmanac.com/world-war-ii.html.
8. Ibid.
9. Cunningham, *New Jersey*, 309
10. "Report Shows New Jersey Is High Producer," *Denville Herald*, January 4, 1940, 8.
11. David Petriello, *Military History of New Jersey* (Charleston, SC: The History Press), 1.
12. Fran Lodry, Carolyn Chermak, Marion Lester, Joan Knapp, Joan Berg, Athena Leonard, interview by author, Denville, February 19, 2020.
13. "Blast," *Denville Herald*, September 12, 1940, 1.
14. Interview by author, February 19, 2020.

15. "Denville Area Escaped Most Blast Tragedy," *Denville Herald*, September 19, 1940, 1.
16. Ibid.
17. "Blast Victim Willing to Return to Powder Plant," *Denville Herald*, September 19, 1940, 1.
18. "Disaster in Small Doses," *Denville Herald*, September 19, 1940, 4.
19. "This Ended…Here," *Denville Herald*, March 21, 1940, 1.
20. Ibid.
21. "Two Robberies," *Denville Herald*, April 18, 1940, 8.
22. Harold Buchanan interview by author, Denville, February 17, 2020.
23. "Banner's House Is Robbed Again," *Denville Herald*, January 11, 1940, 6.
24. "Woman Found After Losing Way in Swamp," *Denville Herald*, August 1, 1940, 8.
25. "Child Found Just in Time," *Denville Herald*, December 27, 1940, 1.
26. "Ox-Drawn Covered Wagon Slows Broadway Traffic," *Denville Herald*, August 8, 1940, 1.
27. "Ballots Now, or Bullets Later," *Denville Herald*, July 25, 1940, 4.
28. "Road to Dictatorship," *Denville Herald*, October 24, 1940, 4.
29. Cunningham, *New Jersey*, 310.
30. "Enlistments in National Guard Urged," *Denville Herald*, September 19, 1940, 4.
31. Ibid.
32. Ibid.
33. "President Roosevelt Signs Selective Training and Service Act," accessed April 14, 2020, https://newspapers.ushmm.org/events/president-roosevelt-signs-selective-training-and-service-act.
34. "Unequal Emphasis," *Denville Herald*, December 5, 1940, 4.
35. "Love Your Enemy—U.S. Style," *Denville Herald*, October 10, 1940, 4.
36. "Selective Service Draft Boards to Sit in School, Library, and Firehouse," *Denville Herald*, October 10, 1940, 1.
37. "The Draft Board Wants to See You," accessed April 14, 2020, https://sos.oregon.gov/archives/exhibits/ww1/Pages/home-front-draft-board.aspx.
38. "Draft Advisory Boards Organized to Assist in Questionnaire Answers," *Denville Herald*, November 14, 1940, 1.
39. "County Draft Quota Likely Easy to Fill," *Denville Herald*, November 20, 1940, 1.
40. "She Does Her Shopping in Denville," *Denville Herald*, February 19, 1943, 3.
41. "Party Well Attended," *Denville Herald*, February 9, 1940, 2.
42. "Christmas Is Observed by Businessmen," *Denville Herald*, December 19, 1940, 10.
43. "Unclassified Column," *Denville Herald*, December 19, 1940, 10.
44. Cunningham, *New Jersey*, 310.
45. "Denville Man Who Was at Pearl Harbor Recognized," unidentified newspaper article, December 4, 1991.

46. Harold Buchanan interview, February 17, 2020.

Chapter 2

47. "Remember Pearl Harbor," poem by Anna Armbruster, *Denville Herald*, January 8, 1942, 2.
48. "Wardens, Police See War Pictures," *Denville Herald*, January 16, 1942, 1.
49. "Now the U.S. Must Fight for Its Life," *LIFE* 2, no. 9, March 2, 1942, 15.
50. "Six Ways to Invade U.S.," *LIFE* 2, no. 9, March 2, 1942, 16.
51. Jonathan Harris, *The Homefront: America During World War II* (New York: G.P. Putnam and Sons, 1984), 63.
52. "Importance of Civilians in Defense Is Emphasized," *Denville Herald*, May 27, 1943, 1.
53. Ibid.
54. Ibid.
55. "Aliens Leave Banned Goods," *Denville Herald*, January 8, 1942, 1.
56. "No Alien Radios or Cameras Here, *Denville Herald*, January 15, 1942, 2.
57. "A Painless Sample," *Denville Herald*, December 14, 1944, 4.
58. Ibid.
59. "Local Defense Council Plans Public Meeting to Explain Its Work," *Denville Herald*, April 16, 1942, 1.
60. "Local Defense Council Gives Full Report," *Denville Herald*, May 14, 1942, 1.
61. Ibid.
62. "Put Your Pails Out," *Denville Herald*, June 4 1942, 4.
63. "Civil Defense Members Win Many Praises," *Denville Herald*, January 7, 1943, 1.
64. "Air Warden's Dance," *Denville Herald*, September 10, 1942, 8.
65. "Wardens Ask for Supplies," *Denville Herald*, October 22, 1942, 1.
66. "Air Spotters to Note More Plan Details," *Denville Herald*, November 26, 1942, 1.
67. "Air Raid Test," *Denville Herald*, January 29, 1942, 1.
68. "What to Do in an Event of an Air Raid," accessed April 21, 2020, https://njdigitalhighway.org/lesson/ww_ii_and_nj/air_raid.
69. "When You Hear an Air-Raid Warning; Don't Telephone," *Denville Herald*, February 6, 1943, 4.
70. Official Air Raid Signals Poster by the Department of Defense State of New Jersey
71. "Give—It's Needed," *Denville Herald*, September 24, 1942, 4.
72. "Recent Test Show Weaker Points in CD," *Denville Herald*, October 8, 1942, 1.
73. Ibid.
74. "Raid Warning Signals Are to Be Altered," *Denville Herald*, January 28, 1943, 1.
75. "Blackout Information," *Denville Herald*, April 23, 1942, 1.
76. Ibid.
77. "Blackout Test Is Successful in Denville," *Denville Herald*, April 30, 1942, 1.

78. Ibid.

79. "Gauer Certain We Are Ready," *Denville Herald*, June 4, 1942, 5.

80. "Blackout May Be Dangerous to You," *Denville Herald*, May 14, 1942, 4.

Chapter 3

81. Jonathan Harris, *The Homefront: America During World War II* (New York: G.P. Putnam's Sons, 1984), 64.

82. "Home Front Must Perform Its Part in Winning War," *Denville Herald*, June 10, 1943, 1.

83. Walter LaFaber, *The American Century* (New York: M.E. Sharpe, 2008), 226.

84. "Some Oil Fuel Questions," *Denville Herald*, October 1, 1942, 4.

85. "Fuel Ration Order Poses a New Problem," *Denville Herald*, December 31, 1942, 1.

86. "Thoughts on Coal," *Denville Herald*, December 2, 1943, 4.

87. "Coal Arrives Just in Time, School Keeps," *Denville Herald*, January 20, 1944, 1.

88. Ibid.

89. "Officials Bring Hopes for Temporary Relief of Local Coal Crisis," *Denville Herald*, January 20, 1944, 1.

90. Ibid.

91. "Office of Price Administration Begins to Ration Automobile Tires," accessed April 25, 2020, https://www.history.com/this-day-in-history/office-of-price-administration-begins-to-ration-automobile-tires.

92. "Mattresses Box Springs," *Denville Herald*, May 21, 1942, 7.

93. "It's Patriotic to Use up Remnants," *Denville Herald*, December 24, 1942, 5.

94. "No Cigarette Rations—No Cigarettes, Either," *Denville Herald*, August 9, 1945, 4.

95. "Four Mothers Made Lunches," *Denville Herald*, March 4, 1943, 1.

96. Harris, *Homefront*, 64.

97. OPA Inspectors Must Have Vigorous Sense of Humor," *Denville Herald*, March 4, 1943, 1.

98. Ibid.

99. "New Member Named to Tire Ration Board," *Denville Herald*, January 8, 1942, 1.

100. "Big Drop in Cars on Road Likely Effect of Ration," *Denville Herald*, January 2, 1942, 1.

101. Ibid.

102. "When Is a Gas Card N.G.? A. When There's No Gas," *Denville Herald*, June 25, 1942, 1.

103. "Dairies Are Hard Hit by ODT Rations," *Denville Herald*, December 3, 1942, 1.

104. "Rationing for the War Effort," accessed April 29, 2020, https://www.nationalww2museum.org/students-teachers/student-resources/research-starters/take-closer-look-ration-books.

105. "Cutting Your Food Costs," *Denville Herald*, February 12, 1942, 6.

106. "Daily Point Budget Record," *Denville Herald*, May 20, 1943, 6.

107. "How to Buy Meat," *Denville Herald*, February 4, 1943, 4.

108. "Canned Ham and Eggs Is Newest Food to Be Sold," *Denville Herald*, April 15, 1943, 7.

109. Harold Buchanan interview, February 17, 2020.

110. D. McDonald, A. Baggot, E. Cougle and M. Kelly, interview by author, Denville, January 27, 2020.

111. "Fireside Tavern," *Denville Herald*, June 11, 1942, 9.

112. Interview by author, January 27, 2020.

113. Harris, *Homefront*, 64.

114. "Your Home and Mine," *Denville Herald*, July 23, 1942, 2.

115. "Rev. Gariss Made Victory Garden Head," *Denville Herald*, March 23, 1943, 1.

116. Ibid.

117. "Thief Again at Gearhart Station," *Denville Herald*, August 31, 1944, 8.

118. "Gas Coupon Theft Creates Interest," *Denville Herald*, September 3, 1942, 1.

119. "Stealing Gas Coupons Cost Thief Only $9," *Denville Herald*, September 17, 1942, 8.

120. "Gives Rules for Drivers," *Denville Herald*, January 1944, 5.

Chapter 4

121. "The Financial Facts You Never Learned about World War II," Money Wise, accessed May 4, 2020, https://moneywise.com/a/financial-facts-about-world-war-ii.

122. Ibid.

123. "Bomb 'em with Junk," *Denville Herald*, August 20, 1942, 2.

124. "Saving 'Scrap' Is Everyone's Job Today," *Denville Herald*, May 28, 1942, 2.

125. "Get your Scrap Ready," *Denville Herald*, September 17, 1942, 4.

126. "Young Mountain of Junk Follows Appeal for Scrap," *Denville Herald*, October 1, 1942, 1.

127. "Junk Drive," *Denville Herald*, October 1, 1942, 1.

128. "Children Gather Local Scrap Pile," *Denville Herald*, September 24, 1942, 8.

129. Ibid.

130. Al Sipple, interview by author, Denville, April 29, 2020.

131. "School Rifle Club Practice," *Denville Herald*, April 1, 1943, 5.

132. "Sixty Bushels of Cans Saved for Tin Drive," *Denville Herald*, February 11, 1943, 1.

133. "Salvage and Stamp Sales in Operation," *Denville Herald*, September 30, 1943, 1.

134. "Scout Troop Contributes Fifty Percent," *Denville Herald*, May 7, 1942, 8.

135. "Say It to a Mirror," *Denville Herald*, January 4, 1945, 4.

136. "Congratulations, Folks on Your Salvage Record," *Denville Herald*, January 4, 1945, 4.

137. "Flash! Flash! Boys and Girls," *Denville Herald*, August 10, 1944, 5.

138. "Emphasis on National Necessity as Denville Theatre Opened Fifth Anniversary Celebration," *Denville Herald*, July 30, 1942, 1.

139. "Write Your Name on a Bomb at the Denville Theatre," *Denville Herald*, June 15, 1944, 5.

140. Ibid.

141. W.J. Rorabaugh, *America: A Concise History* (Belmont, CA: Wadsworth, 1994), 523.

142. "Buy Bonds," *Denville Herald*, August 20, 1942, 1.

143. "What You Buy with War Bonds," *Denville Herald*, May 21, 1942, 8.

144. "Minute Men to Visit Every Home in Denville in U.S. War Bond Drive," *Denville Herald*, August 20, 1942, 1.

145. "Minute Man Drive Got 500 War Bond Pledges," *Denville Herald*, October 1, 1942, 5.

146. "Scouts' Drive to Sell Bonds Shows Results," *Denville Herald*, September 17, 1944, 1.

147. Ibid.

148. "So You Can't Buy Another Bond?" *Denville Herald*, February 17, 1944, 6.

149. "Another Big Bond Sold in Denville," *Denville Herald*, November 22, 1944, 1.

150. "War Bond Stamp Book from WWII, Museum of American Finance," accessed May 7, 2020, https://www.moaf.org/exhibits/checks_balances/franklin-roosevelt/war-bond-stamp-book.

151. Ibid.

152. "Vacation Hit Stamp Buying," *Denville Herald*, January 7, 1943, 6.

153. "War Savings Purchases Up Over $4,000," *Denville Herald*, April 8, 1943, 1.

154. "Near $2 Million in Stamp Sales," *Denville Herald*, July 12, 1945, 8.

155. "Announcing the Morris County War Chest," *Denville Herald*, June 11, 1942, 7.

156. "Chest Gifts Drop Behind Quota Fixed," *Denville Herald*, October 1, 1942, 1.

157. "How Big Is Your Heart?" *Denville Herald*, October 14, 1943, 3.

158. "Gifts to War Chest Fight On 3 Fronts," *Denville Herald*, September 28, 1943, 1.

159. "World War II and the American Red Cross," Red Cross, accessed May 7, 2020, https://www.redcross.org/content/dam/redcross/National/history-wwii.pdf.

160. "Request for Home Nurses," *Denville Herald*, February 19, 1942, 1.

161. "Residents Give 107 Pints to Red Cross Blood Work," *Denville Herald*, July 2, 1942, 3.

162. "Local Persons Donate Blood; Harold Farrand Qualifies for the Membership in Donor Gallon Club," *Denville Herald*, August 10, 1944, 1.

163. "Profit from Show Given By Children Reaches $3," *Denville Herald*, September 10, 1942, 1.

164. "West Morris County Sent Many Products into Battle," *Denville Herald*, August 30, 1945, 1.

165. Ibid.

166. Ibid.

167. "Part Time Employment Opportunity for Vital War Work," *Denville Herald*, November 18, 1943, 8.

168. "Men, Men, Men, Hundreds of Choice Jobs," *Denville Herald*, December 21, 1944, 10.

169. "Arsenal Seeking Soldiers' Rooms," *Denville Herald*, March 1, 1945, 8.

170. "You Have a Cash Asset under Your Roof," *Denville Herald*, March 19, 1942, 5.

171. "Denville Men Share in Picatinny Cash Awards," *Denville Herald*, August 2, 1942, 8.

172. Athena Leonard interview by author, Denville, New Jersey, February 17, 2020.

173. "Aircraft Radio Corporation," accessed May 8, 2020, https://www.radiomuseum.org/dsp_hersteller_detail.cfm?company_id=11006.

174. Elizabeth Hardy interview conducted by author, Denville, NJ, May 12, 2020.

175. Claire (Zieger) Patterson, memoir, Denville (part of Henry Patterson's private collection).

Chapter 5

176. Harris, *Homefront*, 115.

177. Patricia Chappine, *New Jersey Women in World War II* (Charleston, SC: The History Press, 2015), 26.

178. "Help Wanted Ad," *Denville Herald*, July 26, 1945, 4.

179. "Young Women Are Asked to Register Now," *Denville Herald*, April 23, 1942, 1.

180. Ibid.

181. Ibid.

182. "War Jobs for Mothers?," *Parents*, February 1943, 17.

183. Ibid.

184. "Local Woman Takes Over Gas Station Job," *Denville Herald*, April 1, 1943, 1.

185. "Woman Takes Her Own Life," *Denville Herald*, April 1, 1943, 1.

186. "Local Woman's Services Held," *Denville Herald*, February 5, 1942, 8.

187. "Have You a Hidden Talent?" *Denville Herald*, February 24, 1944, 8.

188. "WAAC Takes Denville Girl," *Denville Herald*, July 30, 1942, 1.

189. "War Jobs for Mothers?," 34.

190. "Men and Women in Service, *Denville Herald*, June 24, 1943, 2.

191. "WAC Recruit Campaign is Started Here," *Denville Herald*, November 11, 1943, 1.

192. "Denville Theatre Will Take WAC Applications," *Denville Herald*, May 11, 1944, 1.

193. "Mothers and Daughters to Dine Monday," *Denville Herald*, May 11, 1944, 1.

194. "Bugs, Snakes, Rats—She Begins to Find Them Cute," *Denville Herald*, July 13, 1944, 1.

195. "Work of Red Cross Brings WACs Praise," *Denville Herald*, June 1, 1944, 1.

196. "Woman's Club Tea," *Denville Herald*, March 16, 1944, 4.

197. "Unclassified," *Denville Herald*, August 24, 1944, 4.

198. Harris, *Homefront*, 189.

199. Ibid.

200. Ibid.

201. "Home Found for Infant Left in Pew," *Denville Herald*, December 30, 1943, 1.

202. Ibid.

Chapter 6

203. "Killed in Action," *Denville Herald*, January 8, 1942, 4.

204. "Draft Registry Gains 325 Here," *Denville Herald*, February 19, 1942, 1.

205. "Selectees Are Remembered in Denville," *Denville Herald*, March 19, 1942, 1.

206. "Farewell Is Planned for Local Boys," *Denville Herald*, April 9, 1942, 1.

207. "Bataan Death March," accessed May 15, 2020, https://www.history.com/topics/world-war-ii/bataan-death-march.

208. "Reports Local Boy Missing in War Action," *Denville Herald*, July 2, 1942, 6.

209. "Local Boys in Service," *Denville Herald*, July 23, 1942, 4.

210. Al Sipple interview, April 29, 2020.

211. Henry Patterson interview by author, Denville, January 2020.

212. "Local Boys in Service," *Denville Herald*, June 3, 1943, 1.

213. Ibid.

214. Russell Darpa interview by author, Denville, February 3, 2020.

215. "Memorial War Service Is Approved," *Denville Herald*, September 3, 1942, 1.

216. Gerald A. Danzer, *The Americans* (New York: Holt McDoughal, 2012), 776.

217. "Torpedoed Ship Survivor Describes Attack by Sub," *Denville Herald*, July 23, 1942, 1.

218. Danzer, *Americans*, 778.

219. "Purple Heart to Fennimore," *Denville Herald*, October 7, 1943, 1.

220. "News of Our Men and Women in Uniform," *Denville Herald*, December 28, 1943, 1.

221. "Enemy Observed Rules of Civilized War Against U.S," *Denville Herald*, September 28, 1943, 1.

Chapter 7

222. Danzer, *Americans*, 776.

223. "Local Boy Was Under Fire during Normandy Invasion," *Denville Herald*, November 22, 1944, 1.

224. Al Sipple interview, April 29, 2020.

225. "2 Invasions among King's Experiences in U.S. Navy," *Denville Herald*, September 21, 1944, 1.

226. Henry Patterson interview by author, Denville, NJ January 28, 2020.

227. "2 Invasions among King's Experiences in U.S. Navy" *Denville Herald*, July 1944, 1.

228. Henry Patterson interview, Denville, January 2020.

229. Darpa interview.

230. "D-Day Prayer Service to Be Held in Broadway in Morning of Invasion," *Denville Herald*, May 18, 1944, 1.

Chapter 8

231. "Let's Hope," poem by Olive Morris, *Denville Herald*, October 29, 1942, 3.

232. "News of Our Men and Women in Uniform," *Denville Herald*, August 12, 1943, 4.

233. "Awarded Medal," *Denville Herald*, November 18, 1943, 1.

234. "World War II Bombings Were So Powerful They Sent Shockwaves to Space," https://www.history.com/news/world-war-ii-allied-bombings-shockwaves-space, accessed May 18, 2020.

235. Ibid.

236. "WWII Statistics," Spitfire Association, accessed May 18, 2020, http://pippaettore.com/Horrific_WWII_Statistics.html.

237. "Gets Air Medal," *Denville Herald*, November 9, 1943, 1.

238. "Air Medal Is Given Tustin of 12th A.F." *Denville Herald*, December 28, 1944, 1.

239. "He Keeps 'em Flying," *Denville Herald*, November 9, 1944, 4.

240. "Samuels Given Citation and Higher Rank," *Denville Herald*, November 30, 1944, 1.

241. Ibid.

242. Danzer, *Americans*, 780.

243. Ibid.

244. "Parents Told Austin Minor Listed Killed," *Denville Herald*, November 16, 1944, 1.

245. Ibid.

246. "Local Boys on Casualty List," *Denville Herald*, January 18, 1945, 1.

247. "Pvt. Roleson Killed Jan. 16," *Denville Herald*, February 8, 1945, 5.

248. "Church Memorial for Pvt. Roleson," *Denville Herald*, March 15, 1945, 1.

249. "Cedar Lake Boy Dead in Germany," *Denville Herald*, April 5, 1945, 1.

250. "Bronze Star for Pvt. Mooney Jr.," *Denville Herald*, March 1, 1944, 1.

251. "News of Our Men and Women in Uniform," *Denville Herald*, March 1, 1944, 1.

252. "John Harm Helped Finish Nazi Tank," *Denville Herald*, June 28, 1945, 1.

253. "Hirschi Awarded the Bronze Star," *Denville Herald*, August 2, 1945, 4.

254. "Tabor Soldier Is Given Bronze Star," *Denville Herald*, August 9, 1945, 5.

255. "Arthur Strathman Wins Bronze Star," *Denville Herald*, October 4, 1945, 1.

256. "Reiley Saw How Destitute France Is for Food, Soap," *Denville Herald*, November 21, 1945, 1.

257. "Why Bother?," *Denville Herald*, June 14, 1945, 4.

258. "McCarter Is Prisoner of German Army," *Denville Herald*, November 30, 1944, 1.

259. "Ex-War Prisoner Returns After Three Years Abroad," *Denville Herald*, June 14, 1945, 1.

260. "Promotion and Decoration Awarded to George Blaine," *Denville Herald*, October 4, 1945, 1.

261. "They Made Life Miserable for Romanian Authorities," *Denville Herald*, December 14, 1944, 1.

262. "Home from England, He's Expecting Wife to Follow," *Denville Herald*, October 19, 1944, 1.

263. "Band of Sisters," *New York Times*, accessed May 20, 2020, https://www.nytimes.com/2008/07/06/nyregion/thecity/06brid.html.

264. Winn Hill interview by author, Denville (via phone), April 21, 2020.

Chapter 9

265. Danzer, *Americans*, 785.

266. John Newman, *United States History* (New York: Amsco Publication, 2004), 531.

267. Donald L. Miller, *D-Days in the Pacific* (New York: Simon & Schuster, 2005), 376.

268. "Sgt. Raymond Caporaso Highly Praised for Actions Against Guadalcanal Japs," *Denville Herald*, June 3, 1943, 1.

269. "News of Our Men and Women in Uniform," *Denville Herald*, January 20, 1944, 4.

270. "News of Our Men and Women in Uniform," *Denville Herald*, February 24, 1944, 5.

271. "Sgt. Shaffer Is Discharged After 56 Months in Service," *Denville Herald*, October 11, 1945, 1.

272. "World War II: The U.S. 32nd Infantry Division," accessed May 22, 2020, https://www.historynet.com/world-war-ii-the-us-32nd-infantry-division-battle-to-control-the-villa-verde-trail.htm.

273. "Coykendall, Now in Japan, Had 13,000 Combat Hours," *Denville Herald*, November 29, 1945, 1.

274. "News of Our Men and Women in Uniform," *Denville Herald*, August 26, 1943, 4.

275. "New Flight Officers," *Denville Herald*, August 17, 1944, 1.

276. "Air Medal and DFC Awarded to Local Boy," *Denville Herald*, May 25, 1944, 1.

277. "S/Sgt. Leonard Davenport Home with DFC, Air Medal," *Denville Herald*, August 31, 1944, 1.

278. "Seabee and SoPac Pals," *Denville Herald*, August 3, 1944, 1.

279. "Union Hill Seabee Relates Experiences for Chamber," *Denville Herald*, August 17, 1944, 1.

280. Danzer, *Americans*, 789.

281. Ibid.

282. "Dick McNally Comes Safely Through Iwo Jima Invasion," *Denville Herald*, March 29, 1945, 1.

283. "Can Trust Only Dead Japs," *Denville Herald*, April 20, 1945, 1.

284. "Denville Boy Was Sketching on Iwo," *Denville Herald*, April 12, 1945, 6.

285. Danzer, *Americans*, 789.

286. Ibid.

287. "Bronze Star Give to Tabor Man," *Denville Herald*, September 18, 1945, 8.

288. "Tabor Boy Was in Naha Among First," *Denville Herald*, May 24, 1945, 5.

Chapter 10

289. "They Had a Job to Do," *Denville Herald*, November 1, 1945, 2.

290. "Services Held for V-E Day, *Denville Herald*, May 10, 1945, 1.

291. "Would You," *Denville Herald*, August 9, 1945, 1.

292. "Center Scene of Rejoicing Over Victory," *Denville Herald*, August 17, 1945, 1.

293. Ibid.

294. "Re-Opening April 5th, of the Denville Grill," *Denville Herald*, April 5, 1945, 8.

295. "Cornell's to Open Sunday," *Denville Herald*, November 15, 1945, 1.

296. "Happy Days Are Here Again," *Denville Herald*, August 23, 1945, 5.

297. "Now on Display," *Denville Herald*, November 29, 1945, 3.

298. "MSA Adopts Constitution After Debate," *Denville Herald*, August 10, 1944, 1.

299. C.M. toeLaer, *Bridging the Years in Denville* (Denville, NJ: Haase Publications, 1963), 148.

300. "Looking Ahead," *Denville Herald*, April 5, 1945, 3.

301. "Denville Post Protests Cuts at Picatinny," *Denville Herald*, October 18, 1945, 1.

302. "We've Got the Rope," *Denville Herald*, August 17, 1945, 4.

303. Cunningham, *New Jersey*, 318.

304. Ibid.

305. Ibid.

Epilogue

306. "Our Sincere Wish," *Denville Herald*, December 27, 1945, 4.

ABOUT THE AUTHOR

Peter Zablocki is an author, researcher, teacher and the cohost of the *History Teachers Talking* podcast. Focusing on local history, he is the author of *Denville Goes to War: Denville's Story of World War One* and *Denville 13: Murder, Redemption & Forgiveness in Small-Town New Jersey*, as well as the forthcoming *58 Days of Terror over Elizabeth: Three Airplane Crashes and the Fight to Save Newark Airport*. Peter serves as the vice-president of the Denville Historical Society and Museum and is one of Denville's town historians. He lives with his wife and two sons in Denville, New Jersey.